# YOUR CAREER IN THE

# MEDIA & CREATIVE INDUSTRIES

# YOUR CAREER IN THE

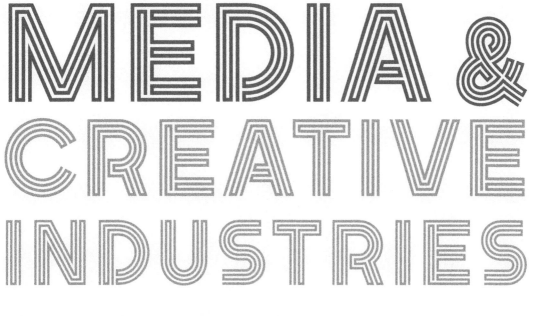

# MEDIA & CREATIVE INDUSTRIES

## BUILDING EMPLOYABILITY SKILLS

MATTHEW KERRY AND GEORGIA STONE

1 Oliver's Yard
55 City Road
London EC1Y 1SP

2455 Teller Road
Thousand Oaks, California 91320

Unit No 323-333, Third Floor, F-Block
International Trade Tower Nehru Place
New Delhi 110 019

8 Marina View Suite 43-053
Asia Square Tower 1
Singapore 018960

Editor: Natalie Aguilera
Editorial Assistant: Sarah Moorhouse
Production Editors: Neelu Sahu and Tanya Kapoor
Copyeditor: Sarah Bury
Proofreader: Christine Bitten
Indexer: KnowledgeWorks Global Ltd
Marketing Manager: Elena Asplen
Cover Design: Francis Kenney
Typeset by KnowledgeWorks Global Ltd
Printed in the UK

**Library of Congress Control Number: 2023938648**

**British Library Cataloguing in Publication data**

A catalogue record for this book is available from the British Library

ISBN 978-1-5297-9652-0
ISBN 978-1-5297-9651-3 (pbk)

At Sage we take sustainability seriously. Most of our products are printed in the UK using responsibly sourced papers and boards. When we print overseas we ensure sustainable papers are used as measured by the Paper Chain Project grading system. We undertake an annual audit to monitor our sustainability.

# CONTENTS

# ABOUT THE AUTHORS

**Matthew Kerry** is a lecturer and Course Leader in Media Production at Nottingham Trent University.

**Georgia Stone** is the School Employability Manager for Arts and Humanities and a lecturer in Media at Nottingham Trent University.

Between them, they have 50 years of combined experience of teaching and preparing students for careers in the media and creative industries.

# PREFACE

## How to Use This Book

This book serves as a core text for your undergraduate media course – especially where you are required to undertake work experience as part of the course. It follows on from *Introducing Media Practice: The Essential Guide,* by the same authors, which brings together the analytical and practical elements of media studies around practical media project work. We see media projects as an opportunity for work experience and the development of skills, qualities and behaviours, and accessing the media and creative industries as a career area.

This sister/companion textbook focuses on using your media degree to access your career. The focus is on developing employability skills while on your degree course, largely through work experience, placements and internships, and through developing a range of good quality employability materials, such as an appropriate CV, social media branding and a career plan. It aims to help you access the media and creative industries using the skills, knowledge and experience built through your media degree course.

The exercises in this book can be used to build a portfolio of career materials that will be of direct use in enhancing your employability. You will also learn from quotes from employers and placement providers with tips and hints about how to approach work experience and career planning. Additionally, you will benefit from the experience of media students and alumni of media studies degrees about their work experience and of entering the world of work in the media and creative industries.

Important terms are highlighted in the Glossary and written in bold the first time they appear in the book. This will enable you to identify and learn specific employability terms and definitions.

# ACKNOWLEDGEMENTS

Thanks to the media degree alumni, media degree students and work experience placement providers for their top tips and hints used throughout this book.

Adrian Abbott, Frederick Bravey, Ben Cook, Ed Corteen, Alexa Garcia Degante, Emily May Drummond, Simon Elliott, Patricia Francis, Jacob Germany, Michael Goulding, Em Green, Stephan Hayward, Millie Hegarty, Shakirah Jelley, Eugene Kogut, Rebecca Lewis, Kyle Lord, Liv Louis, Marco Murru, Ben Newth, Louis Nunn, Zachary Omitowoju, Ebony Pascall, Sam Reynolds, Callum Roome, Tamara Samuel, Laura Savage, Noushka Seher, Megan Shore, Radha Singh, Nikolas Sklinidjis, Emma Snow, Dick Stone, Kennis Tang, Mr Tibbins, Tom Walters, Shauna Wilkinson, Richard Woods

Thank you to our students and colleagues at Nottingham Trent University, including NTU Employability.

Many thanks to Natalie Aguilera, Michael Ainsley, and all at Sage who have helped us through the process of writing this book.

# INTRODUCTION

## Overview of this Book

This book will help you to understand the value of carrying out work experience as part of your media degree, paving your way to accessing the media and creative industries as a career area. The types of careers that are defined by the media and creative industries has broadened significantly over the past few years and continues to do so, due to changes in technology and the escalation of social media. This book acknowledges the wide variety of careers that arts and media students can go into upon graduation and will help you to research the sector.

Historically, careers development has been sidelined on degree courses as an extra-curricular activity, provided by a small team of dedicated staff at universities and colleges. More recently, however, employability has become embedded in the curriculum. You are most probably reading this book because you are studying on a creative media course that includes an element of **work experience**. Your course might have dedicated **work placement** modules, or you might be studying modules where your project briefs are supplied by a client.

Work experience at university is included on almost every type of media degree course, whether it has a vocational remit or not. This book sees work experience placements and course content as an opportunity for developing your employability skills, qualities and attributes.

## Employability Skills and Work Experience

Helyer and Lee (2014) argue that the meaning of the term 'employability skills' ranges between 'skills essential to obtaining a job, such as interview techniques, job-searching skills and those required to create a professional *curriculum vitae*' to essential skills required to effectively accomplish a job, including:

- Generic abilities – teamwork, organisational and communication skills
- Personal attributes – punctuality, self-confidence, discipline and adherence to deadlines
- Specific/subject abilities – skills specific to a particular role, job or career sector

(Helyer and Lee, 2014: 349)

All of the above are explored in this book. Importantly, however, we don't simply list these skills and instruct you how to develop them. Instead, we point out areas where you may already have acquired these skills during your studies or in extra-curricular activities and suggest ways you can enhance them in readiness for undertaking a placement or preparing for graduate-level employment.

Work experience during your course is an important factor in building your professional persona, as are the series of tasks and exercises set out in this book. Having the opportunity to practise your professional skillsets during your time at university will enable you to build confidence and gain an insight into your chosen career sector.

As you work through this book you will be assisted in building your professional persona and employability skills through research into sectors, job roles, networks and support organisations. You will also acquire the vocabulary and confidence that will stand you in good stead for interviews, pitching and working with potential employers and clients.

The book focuses on details such as preparing for work placements, applying and interviewing, modelling your professional behaviour in the workplace, and reflecting on work experience. You are guided towards the world of work through creating a range of good quality career materials, such as an appropriate CV, professional branding and a portfolio.

A series of quotes throughout the book will give you a first-hand insight into the experience of fellow media students, graduates and employers about the benefits of undertaking work experience as part of your studies and where this experience has led them to employment in the media and creative industries.

## The Structure of this Book

We move in a logical progression from thinking about your degree course and what knowledge and skills you have developed to take you into the world of work. From this we support you in the production of employability materials. We offer advice and the opportunity to engage with work experience on your degree. This leads to you reflecting on work experience, and finally becoming career ready.

The book is helpfully written in a way that enables you to engage with activities and exercises that support where you are at any time during work experience: before, during and after. The structure of the chapters is as follows:

Chapter 1, *Media Degrees and Career Skills, Qualities and Attributes*, explores where media students go after graduating. It invites you to start to think about what you might do when you graduate. It encourages you to research career destinations of graduates from your course, learn from alumni, and find out what you might do with your degree. You will analyse the key skills, qualities and attributes you are gaining from your media degree, and you will focus on how your own personal values might shape your career ambitions.

Chapter 2, *Exploring the Media and Creative Industries*, enables you to identify potential employment sectors in order for you to identify potential future careers. The information in this chapter will also be useful when looking for a work placement in these career sectors. The exercises included here will help you to research job sectors and job roles within the media and creative industries; they will also help you to explore the trade press, find relevant support networks, and understand the place of trade unions in the sector you are interested in.

Chapter 3, *Analysing Your Skills and Qualities*, helps you to identify what skills and qualities employers are looking for in graduates and for you to identify which skills and qualities are applicable to your chosen career area. Among the exercises in this chapter, you will be able to explore personal career preferences, to examine key transferable skills required for specific areas in the media and creative industries. You will analyse what is required for an entrepreneurial mindset and you will undertake a skills and qualities audit of yourself.

Chapter 4, *Exploring Potential Career Areas*, gives you step-by-step guidance on conducting a career case study. This involves interviewing an employee in the media and creative industries in order to learn from their experience and learn more about potential jobs that you are interested in. We include a guide to formulating questions and include examples of the types of questions you could ask.

Chapter 5, *Working for Yourself*, will help you to consider the options of self-employment, freelancing or entrepreneurship. Much of the work in the media and creative industries is freelance, and this chapter will help you to identify skills you are developing for this type of career path as well as new ones you may require. It will help you to consider the pros and cons of working for yourself and pose the question 'would working for myself suit me?' One of the exercises in this chapter enables you to match skills and qualities developed at university with skills required for working for yourself.

Chapter 6, *Defining Work Experience*, sets out to explain the different types of work experience you could consider while at university and helps to find the right placement for you. You are also asked to consider the benefits of having work experience and are given advice on where you can look for this experience. The exercises in this chapter help you to make an audit of previous work experience you have done and create SMART objectives for your work experience. You are also encouraged to interview a previous placement student on your course to give you some leads into where you can find your own work experience.

Chapter 7, *Developing Materials for Work Experience*, provides guidance on enhancing and tailoring a CV, cover letter or email in readiness for making applications. The exercises in this chapter help you to build your CV, have it peer reviewed and to produce a targeted cover email.

The way you construct your online brand can be a useful tool for presenting yourself to potential employers. Chapter 8, *Building Your Brand for Work Experience*, helps you to develop a bank of materials on various social media platforms to professionalise your brand further. You are encouraged to carry out an analysis of your current online presence and consider conducting a 'social media makeover' to professionalise your online identity. The exercises in this chapter will guide you through this process.

Chapter 9, *Securing your Placement*, assists you with the process of searching for, making applications and interviewing for work experience. You are helped to prepare for and undertake a practice interview and given guidance to develop the art of pitching, which is important for future self-employment. The exercises in this chapter include answering competency-based questions using the STAR(R) technique and preparing for an elevator pitch. The chapter also includes some tips and hints on how to look after your wellbeing while applying and preparing for interviews for a placement.

Chapter 10, *Preparing for Your Work Experience*, helps you to make the transition from a student to a professional, maximising the success of any work experience you undertake. The chapter will also give you some practical pointers to track your progress that will be useful for reflection after the placement. The chapter supports you through further research into the placement provider's organisation in readiness for your work experience, encourages you to consider your professional identity during your time on the placement, and offers guidance on your health and wellbeing in preparation for the placement.

Chapter 11, *Getting the Best Out of Your Work Experience*, gives an insight into workplace skills that are relevant to many roles and areas of the sector. The chapter discusses the importance of personal skills, such as people skills, communication skills and leadership skills, as well as a range of functional skills that will help you be more effective in your job, such as organisation and time management. The chapter encourages you to analyse and reflect on the professional behaviours that you already have and examine some of the techniques you can use to increase your efficiency and effectiveness in the workplace. Exercises in this chapter include observing colleagues' approach to communication and interpersonal skills as a way of modelling your professional behaviour.

Chapter 12, *Reflecting on Work Experience*, will enable you to contemplate on your work experience in the form of a reflective report or essay. You are encouraged to go through a debrief after your placement, considering the successful and less successful elements of your experience and how to learn from these. You are also given advice on how to approach your placement provider for a reference. The exercises in this chapter include producing a reflective report on work experience, writing a critical reflection essay on work experience and updating your professional branding. The latter is important, as you can include details of your work experience and the skills you have gained from this experience to enhance your online profile.

Finally, Chapter 13, *Preparing for Graduation*, guides you through making preparations for graduating. The chapter supports you in writing a career plan. It outlines the benefits of having a plan and provides a step-by-step guide to helping you create it. You are encouraged to assess your skills and interests, set career goals and develop a plan of action.

By the end of this book, you should have:

- knowledge of the breadth of the employment market that requires media skills and an overview of the many career areas you could pursue
- an understanding of what your future career path might look like and have begun to think about how you might access it
- an understanding of the importance of having a professional digital presence
- an ability to analyse key skills and identify transferrable skills and use these in job applications
- confidence in carrying out a wide range of careers searches and knowing where to look for the sorts of jobs that you aspire to
- produced a good quality CV, portfolio, website, media showreel and professional social media network profile that can be used to support future job applications

This introduction has revealed the contents, aims and structure of the book. It has emphasised the relevance of work experience and working on enhancing your employ-ability as part of your media degree course.

Let's get started!

## Further Reading

Helyer, Ruth, and Lee, Dionne (2014, July) 'The role of work experience in the future employability of higher education graduates'. *Higher Education Quarterly*, 68(3), 348–372.

# 1

# MEDIA DEGREES AND CAREER SKILLS, QUALITIES AND ATTRIBUTES

## Thinking About Your Degree Course in the Context of Your Career

## Introduction

It is possible that you are still a couple of years away from graduation but are already starting to think about where your degree course will take you. This chapter will enable you to think about your degree course in the context of your future career and to reveal what employers are looking for from you. In this book we are focusing mainly on degree courses that have a significant amount of media content. For example, media studies degrees with some practical elements, or more vocational media courses. It is recognised that students from a wider range of courses, such as social sciences and business, will also be employed in and suitably qualified to work in the media and **creative industries**. For students on such degree courses the information and exercises in this chapter still apply.

Employers are interested in evidence of certain attributes you will have developed through your degree. Usually, a good degree award is sought but the degree itself is only part of what they are looking for. Employers are also looking for students with relevant experience in the field and in the world of work. They are looking for evidence of transferable skills that can be applied to the career sector you are aiming for. By **transferable skills**, we mean **skills** that you can apply from one context to another, for example, teamwork and interpersonal skills from a university project to a professional workplace.

After reading this chapter you will be able to:

- find out where media students go after graduating
- learn from alumni (graduates) of your course about your potential options
- examine the key skills you will develop through your degree
- consider your personal values and preferences for shaping your career options

List of exercises in this chapter:

- Examining your motivations for a media degree
- Researching career destinations of graduates
- Locating alumni from your course
- Analysing key skills, qualities, attributes and behaviours
- Aligning your personal values with aspirations

# Types of Media Degrees

As we pointed out in the introduction, there are a wide range of degree courses that combine media theory and practice in some way. Most are not necessarily vocational in the sense that they are preparing you for working in specific areas, but it is likely that you will end up pursuing a career in the media and creative industries. A useful place to start is to examine your motivations for applying for the course in the first place.

## Exercise: Examining Your Motivations for a Media Degree

Think back to before you started the course and consider what motivated you to apply for your degree. Use this exercise to identify a burgeoning interest in the media and creative industries and think about how this could lead to a future career. List details of the following:

- What media you consume, such as gaming, podcasts, cinema, streamed content, social media, music, events and festivals, theatre, current affairs, and advertising
- Your hobbies and pastimes that involve you producing media content, for example photography, blogging, social media, travel vlogs, short videos, composing and recording music
- Your media experience to date from previous education, such as coursework assignments and projects
- Any relevant work experience you have gained, such as paid work and self-employment, placements and internships, holiday work and volunteering, including involvement in clubs and societies
- Networks you have built, for example, relatives, friends and social media connections who work in the media and creative industries

Once you have outlined the motivations for applying to your degree course, reflect on this to identify three current general ideas of the sorts of careers that you might want to pursue. There is no pressure here to specify particular jobs or career areas, just an encouragement to think about what is currently sparking your enthusiasm and interest. You may find it easier to think of this in terms of what you don't want to do in order to narrow your focus.

You could use this as the basis of a presentation to your peers, which could give you additional inspiration.

# Where do Media Graduates Go?

Your primary motivation for applying for a media degree was probably your enthusiasm for the subject but you might also have thought about where this type of course could take you in the future. It can be both instructive and inspirational to do some research into the career destinations of previous students on your degree course.

## Thinking About What You Would Like to do When You Graduate

Looking ahead to graduating from your degree and thinking about what your career destination might be, imagine it is the day after the graduation ceremony and the subsequent celebrations. You are no longer a student. You have your whole future ahead of you. Now it is time to enter the 'real' world of work! What plans have you got in place? How will you use your degree to enter that world?

Let's establish where you are currently in the process of considering your future career. Are you fully decided, still deciding, or have you not thought about it at all? What do you think you need to do right now in order to make plans for work post-graduation?

The following exercise will give you the opportunity to research the career destinations of graduates from your degree course.

## Exercise: Researching Career Destinations of Graduates

You can find out where graduates from your degree course go through the Higher Education Careers Service Unit (HECSU) luminate.prospects.ac.uk. From the 'what do graduates do?' page, download the report and find the subject area of your degree from the contents page. This will give you some statistics and information about the career destinations of graduates from your degree course 15 months after graduating. For example, the top ten professions for students from a media studies degree are listed as:

1   Marketing associate professionals
2   Public relations professionals
3   Arts officers, producers and directors
4   Photographers, audio-visual and broadcasting equipment operators
5   Graphics and multimedia designers
6   Human resources and industrial relations officers

7   Business sales executives
8   Business and related research professionals
9   Authors, writers and translators
10  Programmers and software development professionals

(What do graduates do? 2023, luminate.prospects.ac.uk/what-do-graduates-do)

Reflect on the information you have found, thinking especially about anything that has struck you about the potential career areas that you could go into. Of the top ten professional jobs listed, which ones are of interest to you at this moment? Is there anything that has come as a surprise to you in your findings? Are there any that you would like to delve into and find more detail about?

You will use your initial findings here as the basis of further research into specific career sectors and jobs throughout this book.

## Investigating Graduate Outcomes from Your Course

You can follow up this research by investigating the career destinations of students from your own degree course. You can find this information out from your university's careers service and your tutors via the Graduate Outcomes Survey (GOS). This is a questionnaire that goes out to all graduates 15 months after graduation. It gathers information about what jobs or further study the graduates are undertaking. It also asks questions about their current employment or further study situation. For example, they ask to what extent graduates agree with the following statements:

* My current work/study fits in with my future plans
* My current work/study is meaningful
* I am utilising what I learnt during my studies in my current work/study

It will be interesting for you to find out where graduates of your degree are working or studying, but also how they are utilising what they learned on the course.

─( **Hear from the Experts** )──────────────────────────

"I did an undergraduate degree where I earned a 2:1 in (BA) Media and Communication. After graduating, I undertook my first role as a PR intern at a boutique PR agency providing PR and social media services to clients in the B2B [business to business] and B2C [business to consumer] sectors before being promoted to PR executive. I'm now a Senior Digital PR Executive at a search-first creative agency. I deliver brand-building digital PR strategies and campaigns to global household brand names across beauty, home and lifestyle sectors."

– *Tamara Samuel, Senior Digital PR Executive*

"I studied (BA) Media, Communication and Society. Despite graduating with a great degree, I didn't secure my first marketing role until a year after graduation due to the tough economic climate at the time. Marketing roles were in short supply and the industry landscape was incredibly competitive for recent graduates. But persistence paid off and I was fortunate enough to be hired as a Marketing Assistant in the tourism industry. I then pursued an exciting role as an Account Executive for a creative agency. I'd always wanted to work agency-side and I knew the Managing Director from my time as an intern with the business while studying for my degree. Fast forward to today, I am a Director of the agency with the long-term plan to take on the role of Managing Director in the coming years and run the agency in partnership with our Creative Director. So, when I say it's been a whirlwind, I'm not exaggerating!"

*– Tom Walters, Account Director, The Dairy*

## Learning from Alumni

**Alumni** are graduates or former students of your degree course. You can learn a lot from people who have been in your shoes before you. Your course tutors may be able to put you in touch with such people. Most universities have a department that engages with their alumni. They may have pages on the web with profiles of graduates of the university and maybe also an alumni magazine.

## Exercise: Locating Alumni from Your Course

We will be encouraging you to create a profile on **LinkedIn**, a professional social media app, in a later chapter. For the purposes of this exercise, you could sign up with a basic profile for now. You can research alumni from your course via the LinkedIn alumni tool. We will be encouraging you to research and interview alumni in a later chapter, but for now just finding out where they are in terms of their career will be a useful starting point.

Go to LinkedIn.com/alumni and it will recognise your university from your profile. This will take you to the alumni tool for your place of study. In the alumni tab you will be able to:

- see what alumni in your field have accomplished since graduation and expand your sense of what's possible for you
- identify alumni in your field and reach out to them for their industry expertise and career opportunities
- learn about job opportunities and mentoring partnerships

(LinkedIn.com)

What kind of inspiration have you taken from the profile/s you have found?
How do you intend to use this information?
We will revisit your LinkedIn connections and make use of them in future chapters.

# What Can I Do With My Degree?

One place where you can find out what you can do with your degree is on the Prospects website. Visit prospects.ac.uk and look at the section titled 'What can I do with my degree?' to help you explore the possibilities. For example, a search for 'Media Studies' will take you to a wealth of material on job options directly related to the degree, such as:

- Digital marketer
- Media researcher
- Public relations officer
- Social media manager
- Television/film/video producer
- Web content manager

There is also a list of jobs where a media degree would be useful, such as:

- Broadcast journalist
- Event manager
- Film director
- Marketing executive
- Photographer
- UX designer

This is followed by some examples of the typical employment sectors for graduates of media courses:

- Television, radio, and film and video companies
- Communications agencies
- Marketing organisations
- Media companies
- PR consultancies
- Computer games

This is a broad insight to where your media degree could take you. We will be exploring this in more depth at several points later in this book.

# Examining Key Skills, Qualities and Attributes Gained from Media Degrees

A good starting point to exploring where your degree might take you is to consider what transferable skills and knowledge you are developing through your course that will be useful in the workplace. We will consider what skills and qualities employers in the media and creative industries are looking for from graduates in Chapter 3. Here we will focus on the transferable skills you are gaining from your media degree. These align well with the **skills**, **qualities and attributes** sought by media and creative industry employers and also the demands of **self-employment**.

- **Commercial sector awareness** – an attribute for understanding how industries work, what is going on in the world, and how it might impact the future
- **Communication skills** – skills in achieving communicative goals via particular communication behaviours (such as giving oral presentations or composing emails)
- **Creativity and innovation** – an attribute for offering ideas and solutions to challenges from new and unique angles and putting those ideas into action
- **Critical analysis** – a skill in assessing the quality of evidence in scholarship to decide whether it can support your argument
- **Critical reflection** – a skill in thinking objectively about situations and experiences, analysing and learning from them
- **Cultural awareness** – an awareness and acceptance of other cultures and colleagues' cultural identities in the workplace and wider community
- **Entrepreneurship** – a set of skills and attributes related to risk-taking actions in setting up new enterprises for profit. An **enterprising** person will be willing to try out new and unusual ways of achieving something
- **Equality, diversity and inclusion (EDI) awareness** – a quality for recognising and understanding **protected characteristics** (for example, gender, ethnicity, disability, LGBTQ+) and making people feel welcomed and valued
- **Leadership and management** – skills in influencing and motivating others to achieve a common goal
- People/**interpersonal skills** – skills used to communicate and interact with others effectively (such as **active listening**, giving and receiving feedback, emotional intelligence)
- **Problem-solving** – a skill in responding to and managing unexpected situations or challenges
- **Project management** – an attribute for the use of knowledge, skills and techniques to result in a deliverable outcome
- Research – a skill in investigating sources in order to establish facts and reach new conclusions
- **Sustainability awareness** – an attribute for ensuring a balance between economic growth, environmental care and social wellbeing for current and future generations
- **Teamwork** – a skill in working effectively and collaboratively with others
- Technical/practical – skills and proficiency in relevant hardware and software
- **Time management** – a skill in using and organising time productively and efficiently
- **Working to a brief** – a skill in following instructions to a shared purpose
- Writing – a skill in communicating effectively in the written form to different audiences using a variety of registers and purposes

To this list of transferable skills and knowledge developed from your degree, you can add those skills, qualities and attributes derived from taking part in career-relevant work experience, which we will engage with later in this book.

In addition, it is important to appreciate the transferable skills gained through your wider life at university. These include qualities, attributes and **behaviours** enhanced through **extra-curricular** activities; life skills developed through independent living and social activity; and skills and attributes gained through paid work to support your time at university. These sorts of life skills are:

- people skills
- responsibility and self-motivation
- looking after yourself
- budgeting
- overcoming obstacles
- organisation and time management
- confidence building

(prospects.ac.uk)

## Exercise: Analysing Key Skills, Qualities, Attributes and Behaviours

Look at the two lists above and select five of the skills, qualities, attributes and behaviours that strike you as being important. For each one, do the following:

- identify where on your course and/or in your university life they are being utilised and developed
- give some examples from your own experience
- assess the level of competence you feel you currently have
- suggest ways you might improve and further develop the skill, quality, attribute or behaviour
- indicate how it might feature in the world of work or work experience

This is a useful exercise to contribute to the production of your **curriculum vitae (CV)** and professional portfolio in later chapters.

─┤ **Hear from the Experts** ├──────────────────────────────────

"The two most important skills that I gained from my course are probably not the most obvious ones. I would have to say they are problem solving and project management. Working in production management means you are constantly prioritising, knowing what requires immediate attention and finding quick solutions to enable the smooth running of a production and adapting to a fast-paced, changing environment."

*– Ebony Pascall, Production Manager, BBC Children's and Entertainment*

"I'd say fundamentally all of the practical skills that I learned on my course have come into play. That's everything from going out filming and getting hands-on with the equipment and editing as well. I do a lot of editing, so all of the editing experience that I gained on the course is fundamental to what I do now. I don't think I could do my job if I didn't learn all the skills that I did on the course."

*– Sam Reynolds, Video and Motion Producer, Adtrak*

# Your Career Lifespan

It is worth thinking about your career in terms of your whole lifetime. It will begin after you graduate and is likely to take up at least four decades of your life before retirement. It is important therefore that you take a vested interest in considering a career that will excite, enthuse and inspire you for a sustained period of your life.

In order to start thinking about what your career might look like, you can analyse your personality and personal values and how these align with your future work journey.

## Personality

Your personality, and the type of person you feel you are, can determine what type of career you go into. **Personality traits** are different from skills and qualities, which are learned through experience. They are defined by your characteristic feelings and behaviours. Employers often list personality traits in job adverts or look for evidence of them in applications and interviews.

Thinking about the list below, can you identify with any of these personality traits, and how would you define them against yourself?

P – positive
E – empathetic
R – resourceful
S – sociable
O – open-minded
N – nurturing
A – approachable
L – likeable
I – imaginative
T – trustworthy
Y – (be) Yourself!

Employers often use **psychometric tests** in the process of recruiting and interviewing for jobs. One of these tests is generally structured around measuring your personality in terms of your interests, values, beliefs, and your motivations and ways of thinking. Others test your **verbal reasoning** (evaluating the logic of a given statement),

**situational judgement** (how you respond to work-based scenarios) and **strengths** (how you demonstrate the durability required for a particular role).

You can access mock versions of psychometric tests for free through your university careers service or online, and it is worth considering this later in the book when you are preparing for interviews.

## Personal Values

As you are going to be investigating careers in the media and creative industries, it is worth thinking at this stage about what you want to get out of your career in the long run. Thinking about your ethical choices and personal values may influence you to seek out jobs and organisations that you feel have integrity. This in turn will make you think about what you want to get out of work and life. The next exercise will help you to start articulating this.

## Exercise: Aligning Your Personal Values with Aspirations

Look at the list below of some of the questions/considerations you might have about how you want your career to look.

Do some research into these online.

What does the career area you want to go into look like in terms of equality, diversity and inclusion (EDI)? This could involve you in considering issues such as:

- **diversity** of the workforce – the variety of ethnic, socio-economic and cultural backgrounds that people come from
- **pay gaps** – the difference between pay awarded to different sectors of the workforce
- **glass ceiling** – the barriers to career success
- how the profiles of leadership and management are reflected in terms of equality (for example, how any women are in positions of leadership)

To help with your research, you may want to consider the list of nine protected characteristics (in the Equality Act 2010) and how evident they are in the results you find.

1 Age
2 Gender
3 Race
4 Disability
5 Religion or belief
6 Sexual orientation
7 Gender reassignment
8 Marriage or civil partnerships
9 Pregnancy and maternity

Search using terms such as 'media and creative industries diversity', 'media and creative industries inclusion', or 'media and creative industries equality'. This may result in you finding industry reports, government policy documents, and academic/scholarly articles, for instance.

Make some notes on how your research aligns with your own personal values, cultural and social background, and your life/career aspirations. Do any of the results give you optimism for the future? Do any of the results concern you in terms of your own entry into the industry? What might you do to affect change, if required?

Repeat this exercise focusing on other considerations, such as:

- Media and creative industries and sustainability – how the industry ensures a balance between economic growth, environmental care and social wellbeing for current and future generations
- Media and creative industries and **corporate social responsibility (CSR)** – how a company integrates social and environmental concerns to be accountable to its stakeholders

You can also alter your search to be narrower in focus, looking at specific career areas that you might be interested in, for example, the screen industries, marketing or gaming.

In future chapters we will suggest ways to find industry support and support networks within the media and creative industries which will align with your personal values and cultural and social background.

## Hear from the Experts

"I have shaped my career around doing the work that I think is important and worthwhile. I am hired not only because I'm educated and experienced in a variety of different topics, but also [because I] am not afraid to speak my opinions on those subjects and contribute to discussions on the topics we are creating content about. By taking a strong stance and defending those opinions (while being open to other opinions of course!), you are more likely to find your 'tribe' or 'network' and thus find work opportunities through this."

*– Adrian Abbott, self-employed director, producer and editor*

"You don't get points for trying to please everyone because you never will. So, find the things that you actually believe in and stick to them because otherwise you won't find your work fulfilling. Take this from someone who's been around a couple of times in really terrible jobs. Don't compromise on what you believe in because the world tells you to or because of what you're seeing on social media. It's rubbish and there's room for your ideas. So stick to them!"

*– Ben Cook, Digital Designer/Filmmaker*

"In general, just try to be yourself – show your personality because that is most important. And I think the other thing that I would like to mention as well is not to worry too much about what people think of you, because the creative industry is probably the best industry for diversity, for people with weird thoughts and opinions and different lifestyles. And as a member of the LGBT community as well, I was a bit worried going into the industry, I was thinking: how is that going to work? Are people going to accept me? And on the whole they have. It's a really nice industry to be a part of."

*– Em Green, Motion Designer*

"I have a successful freelance career working for many different organisations in the third sector. Everyone would always tell you that you can't live comfortably doing something that you also simultaneously feel ethical about. It's like this societal push to make us all step on each other to get ahead. But ultimately if you value your worth, and your worth has client value, then they will pay you for that. Join a union. Stand side by side with the workers in your sector. If the minimum day rate is an accepted certain cost, don't be a scab and undercut everyone else to be competitive – you just depreciate the total earning power for everyone."

*– Adrian Abbott, self-employed director, producer and editor*

## Summary

In this chapter we have considered your degree course in the context of your future career. We have helped you to look into where media students and alumni of your course go after graduating and to learn from their experience. We have also started to focus on the key skills, qualities, attributes and behaviours you are enhancing through your degree course and analysed how you can use this knowledge in your future development. Finally, we encouraged you to consider your personality traits, personal values and social and cultural background, and how these might shape your career aspirations.

In the next chapter we will give an overview of the media and creative industries to help you to start exploring potential future careers.

## Further Reading

What do graduates do? 2023, luminate.prospects.ac.uk/what-do-graduates-do. This is an annual survey of the career destinations of graduates from all degree courses in the UK.

# 2

# EXPLORING THE MEDIA AND CREATIVE INDUSTRIES

## Identifying Potential Employment Sectors

## Introduction

In the previous chapter you considered your degree course in the context of **employability**. You thought about the transferable skills developed on the course and how this could help you prepare for work after graduation.

In this chapter we are going to explore the media and creative industries in order for you to start identifying potential future careers. The information in this chapter will also be useful when looking for work experience in these career sectors.

Many students from media degrees also go into the areas of journalism, advertising, marketing (especially social media) and PR, and some go into teaching. Some will work for themselves and may have a **portfolio career** (where they work on freelance jobs from a variety of sectors). Lots of 'new' job titles are arising all the time, such as Analytics, Motion Graphics, Digital Content and Social Media Manager. This chapter will consider what it is like to work in the different areas of the media and creative industries and will involve you in researching adverts for jobs currently available in the sector/s you are interested in. We will focus on self-employment separately in Chapter 5.

This chapter will help you to:

- identify what the media and creative industries are
- have an overview of the sectors that make up the media and creative industries
- identify the types of jobs available in the media and creative industries and to examine some case studies
- find out what it is like to work in the media and creative industries

List of exercises in this chapter:

- Researching job sectors within the media and creative industries
- Exploring the trade press
- Learning from sector networks and support organisations
- Understanding the place of trade unions in your sector
- Linking with professional and **trade associations**
- Researching job roles within the media and creative industries
- Aligning your job choices with your personal values and career aspirations

# What are the Media and Creative Industries?

You will have found from your research in Chapter 1 that media students tend to go into a wide range of careers that can be categorised as being in the broad media and creative industries. This will be the focus of this chapter.

Davies and Sigthorsson (2013: 1–2) define the creative industries in the following way:

> The creative industries don't exist – at least not as a unified category. ... we treat the 'creative industries' as an umbrella term that covers a variety of activities, products and services. ... A tremendous range of economic activity arises from the creation of pleasure and meaning. These experiences, when they take the forms of goods and services, provide work for a host of people ranging from computer programmers and engineers to writers, artists and musicians. There are also many kinds of services, from public relations (or PR) to interaction design to retailing, where pleasure, meaning and experience are absolutely central to the business.

The UK Government's Department for Digital, Culture, Media and Sport (DCMS) defines the creative industries as: 'those industries which have their origin in individual creativity, skill and talent and which have the potential for wealth and job creation through the generation and exploitation of intellectual property' (DCMS, 2015)

So, the creative industries are those which have their origin in creativity, skill and talent. Sectors within the creative industries include advertising and marketing, graphic design, fashion design, museums and galleries, film, television, radio, music and performing arts.

Even if people are not directly involved in some of these sectors, it is likely that there may be some crossover at some stage in their career where they work with other people in these fields – a videographer working with a fashion designer, for example, or a web designer working with a musician. You might be interested in one particular sector, but it is worth considering that they are not mutually exclusive. Different sectors will often work together, so it is a good idea to gain a broad insight into what they are. This is worth bearing in mind at this early stage of your career considerations.

---

**Hear from the Experts**

---

"I've got a bit of a holistic view and I think it just makes for a better production in terms of me being able to focus on a specific role and allowing the skilled freelancers to do what they do. We've got storyboard artists on our books. We've got camera operators, editors, motion graphic artists, actors, production assistants, camera operators, producers and voice over artists, so, quite a varied list. There's a good variety and a lot of skilled freelancers, we're probably talking about a pool of 30 people that I can call upon depending on what sort of project. And the good news for you guys is that we're all making a living from media, so you know, there are jobs out there."

*– Ben Newth, Head of Video at a corporate video company*

"Let's just assume the technical skills are there. There are certain skill sets you're going to need to be able to do the job. They all revolve around passion. You know someone that actually wants to be there and wants to do it. Their passion will enthuse people around them and we have a passionate team. We want to build on that passion. It doesn't mean your passion has to be the same as everybody else's. Far from it, the diversity in that is fantastic. Actually, that's what gives you a great project team."

*– Simon Elliott, Managing Director, Diversity Agency*

---

# Researching Sectors in the Creative Industries

A good place to start when looking at this vast area is to break it down into **job sectors** and focus in on particular areas of interest for you. The UK Government's DCMS split the creative industries into the following sectors:

- Advertising
- Architecture
- Art and antiques markets
- Crafts
- Design
- Designer fashion
- Film and video
- Interactive leisure software
- Music
- Performing arts
- Publishing
- Software and computer services
- Television and radio

To this we could also add the Games industry. You can see from the above how many of the sectors of the creative industries are linked to media, which is why this book is focused on the broad area of the media and creative industries.

The following exercise will help you to organise and summarise your research into sectors of the media and creative industries.

## Exercise: Researching Job Sectors Within the Media and Creative Industries

After looking through the websites listed below, choose a specific job sector that is closest to your current career interest area/s. Write a summary of what you have learned from the website/s you have looked at and identify one thing that you *did not know* before reading this material that you will take into your future career research.

On the career sectors pages of Target Jobs (targetjobs.co.uk), you will find links to many career sectors, including:

* Marketing, advertising, PR
* Media, journalism and publishing

On Prospects (prospects.ac.uk), you will find links to:

* Creative arts and design
* Marketing, advertising and PR
* Media and internet
* Games industry

On the Creative Toolkit website of the Broadcasting, Entertainment, Communications and Theatre Union (BECTU) (creativetoolkit.org.uk), you will find pages on:

* Television
* Radio
* Digital media
* Film

---( Hear from the Experts )------------------------------------

"There are so many different jobs in the creative industry that you just don't know about until you step into it a bit further. I didn't know Assignment Editor was a job until I found it. I thought I wanted to be a photographer because I had an interest in photography. But there's so many opportunities, even in sales, marketing and publishing. So do be open minded."

*– Rebecca Lewis, Senior Creative Content Editor, Getty Images*

"If you look at the creative industry, 2.2 million people [are] employed in this industry, 96% of those work in micro-businesses or [are] self-employed, a third are self-employed. That still leaves 63% of the people in our industry who work in companies between two and nine people in size. They're the most entrepreneurial, dynamic, enterprising, exciting places to work that can offer the greatest breadth of experience, the greatest depth of responsibility, only nobody knows as they are so hidden, operating under the radar."

*– Richard Woods, Co-founder, CREATEBritain.com*

# Finding Out What it is Like to Work in the Media and Creative Sector

The reality of working in the media and creative sector can be unexpected and something you should be aware of before committing to this career path. The work can be variable and unpredictable with long hours and difficult working conditions. It can also be a very competitive area to work in as you start at the bottom of the pay scale and work your way up. These are features of working in this sector which might be negative points for some people. Davies and Sigthorsson (2013: 102–103) point out how work in the creative sector can be 'seasonal', built around key events such as trade fairs and festivals. They also highlight that starting out in this type of career may include 'unpaid labour' and that getting a foot in the door 'even for no pay or low pay, can be a hard slog' (Davies and Sigthorsson, 2013: 112).

## Hear from the Experts

"I've worked 70+ hours a week at a chain pub and was absolutely miserable. I was determined to make something more of myself and then moved on to work to someone else's tune at some of the top post-houses in commercial advertising and domestic television documentary work. I was still miserable. I sacrificed living in a fancy house in West London and a high-paying producer job to sleep on floors, in tents, mobile homes and static caravans in order to take editorial photo and video of current events and build a portfolio that I could be proud of."

*– Adrian Abbott, self-employed director, producer and editor*

"I've been working at Framework Design for about five months and I've been learning just so much just from being in the work environment, how it works, how you should behave, all those things. It was very nice to start in the creative industry. It's not super corporate and not super serious."

*– Alexa Garcia Degante, Account Executive, Framework Design*

A revealing way to get a glimpse into what it is like to work in the industry is to look at the **trade unions**, **professional associations**, **trade press**, and networks that support the sector you are interested in. Over the next few pages we present a series of exercises to help you research a number of different creative sectors, and lead into looking at specific job roles.

## Exercise: Exploring the Trade Press

All work sectors have a related trade press. This is usually an online publication that investigates issues to do with the sector. Have a look at the ones below that relate to your interest area and see if you can find any others of your own, especially if you are looking to enter a niche sector.

Make some notes on what these sources tell you about working in your chosen sector of the media and creative industries.

Broadcast/TV/film:

- Bfi.org.uk – an organisation for film in the UK. The British Film Institute (BFI) supports film production, distribution, education and audience development
- Broadcastnow.co.uk – an organisation that supports the broadcast industries, including a monthly magazine
- Cinematography.com – a community providing education, news and resources for cinematographers
- Empireonline.com – an organisation linked to a magazine that reviews films and related areas in the movie world
- Thegotham.com – a community of independent creators, producers and distributors which provides career-building resources and access to the film industry and publishes Filmmakermagazine.com
- Theknowledgeonline.com – a production directory that gives access to information on UK film and TV and provides contact information on crews for productions
- Media.info – a site for media news and jobs worldwide
- Televisual.com – a magazine focusing on the UK production community

Radio:

- Radiotoday.co.uk – news, jobs and events in the radio industry

Marketing:

- Campaignlive.co.uk – an organisation and magazine serving the marketing, advertising and media communities
- Thedrum.com – a publisher for the marketing and media industries with insight and guidance on the sector
- Marketingweek.com – offers the latest marketing news, opinion, trends, jobs and challenges facing the marketing industry

Public relations:

- Prweek.com – a trade magazine for the **public relations** industry with news, analysis and jobs

Publishing:

- Thebookseller.com – a trade magazine and website offering news and job opportunities for employees in the book trade

Games industry:

- mcvuk.com – (MCV/Develop) a UK trade magazine that focuses on the business aspects of the video games industry

## Exercise: Learning from Sector Networks and Support Organisations

Most sectors have networks that offer support and guidance to people working within the sector. Listed below are some examples of **sector networks** and **support organisations** that you can use to complement your own research.

Pick out some examples of networks you might want to join when entering the sector. (Some of them include student membership.) Make some notes about what you have learned from doing this research.

- The Chartered Institute of Marketing (cim.co.uk) – a membership organisation that supports, develops and represents marketers and marketing organisations worldwide
- The Creative Industries Federation (creativeindustriesfederation.com) – a networking and campaigning organisation for the creative industries
- Creative Pool (creativepool.com) – a networking organisation for the creative sector
- Filmtvcharity.org.uk – a charity supporting people working in the film, TV and cinema industry
- The Guild of Television Camera Professionals (gtc.org.uk) – a member organisation for professionals working in all areas of production
- Into Film (intofilm.org) – a network organisation that supports teachers and educators involved in film and media studies
- Mama Youth (mamayouth.org.uk) – a support organisation for young people from diverse communities wanting to enter the media industry
- Media Trust (mediatrust.org) – a charity working with media and community groups
- Production Base (productionbase.co.uk) – a networking organisation for freelancers
- The Production Guild of Great Britain (productionguild.com) – a support/ membership organisation for film and TV drama professionals
- Publishers Association (publishers.org.uk) – a membership organisation for the publishing industry
- The Radio Academy (radioacademy.org) – a networking organisation for people working in radio

- Raisingfilms.com – a discussion space for filmmakers with families
- So You Want to Network – a LinkedIn community to educate and inspire young Black women in marketing and PR
- Soulsound (soulsound.co.uk) – a membership organisation for supporting sound engineers
- thetvcollective.org – a group supporting filmmakers from diverse backgrounds
- TIGA.org – a network for games developers and digital publishers and the trade association representing the video games industry
- Triforce Creative Network (thetcn.com) – a networking organisation and a place to showcase work
- UK Black Comms Network (blackcommsnetwork.co.uk) – a support network that aims to increase the seniority of Black PR and communications professionals in the UK
- Women in Film and Television Network (wftv.org.uk) – a membership organisation supporting women in the media and creative sector

## Hear from the Experts

"The most important network that I'm a part of is the Chartered Institute of Marketing. The CIM is the membership organisation for our industry and offers an in-depth range of qualifications and careers support to those working in marketing. I've been a member of the CIM for many years and I completed my Level 6 CIM Diploma in Strategic Marketing. It's undoubtedly up there with my degree as one of the most important qualifications I've undertaken. I would recommend it to any marketing professionals looking to continue their professional development and further enhance their knowledge. A membership also opens the door to exclusive events and content to further support your career progression so even if a course isn't the right step for you at this moment in time, I would strongly recommend becoming a member."

*– Tom Walters, Account Director, The Dairy*

"I am a member of the UK Black Comms Network and So You Want To Network. I'm also a mentee on Bloom UK's mentoring programme. These industry networks and organisations have allowed me to connect with and seek career advice from inspirational people in the industry."

*– Tamara Samuel, Senior Digital PR Executive*

## Exercise: Understanding the Place of Trade Unions in Your Sector

The different areas of the media and creative industries will belong to different trade unions. Trade unions offer support and advice to people working within their sector. The Trades Union Congress (TUC) has some useful information about what a union is and why you might want to join one when you are in work.

Go to the TUC website (TUC.org). Using the application 'find a union for you', discover which union is most suited to the area you are interested in. You can search using the industry or a job title and it will suggest the most suitable union to join for the industry or job title you input. You may also want to explore student membership of the unions below, as this could be one way into the industry.

Here are some specific unions involved in the different sectors of the media and creative industries:

- Broadcasting, Entertainment, Communications and Theatre Union (BECTU) – a union for people working in the media and entertainment industries, including a branch representing games industry workers
- Equity – a union for performers and creative practitioners
- IWGB Gameworkers – a trade union representing UK gameworkers
- Musicians' Union (MU) – a union for people working in the music industry
- National Union of Journalists (NUJ) – a union for the journalism industry
- Writers Guild (WGGB) – a trade union representing professional writers in all areas

After finding a trade union relevant to your chosen sector, write a short summary about the types of support and membership benefits they could offer you. Pick out any campaigns they are running that are relevant to the sector you are interested in.

## Exercise: Linking with Professional and Trade Associations

Below are some **professional** and **trade associations**. These are similar to trade unions in that they represent their members in specific industry areas. Have a look below at any that relate to your chosen career area. Note that some of these might require you to sign up and pay for membership, which is not recommended while you are a student (unless they have student discount).

- Association of Independent Professionals and the Self Employed (IPSE) – a professional association for the self-employed
- British Interactive Media Association (BIMA) – a professional association for those working in interactive media
- Chartered Institute of Marketing – a professional association for those working in marketing
- Chartered Institute of Public Relations – a professional association for those working in public relations
- Institute of British Advertisers – a professional association for those working in advertising
- Institute of Practitioners in Advertising – a professional association for those working in advertising
- International Moving Image Society – an international community for the moving image industry

- Producers Alliance for Cinema and Television (PACT) – an organisation for independent film and television producers
- Public Relations Consultants Association – a professional association for those working in public relations
- United Kingdom Interactive Entertainment (UKIE) – the trade body for the games and interactive entertainment industry

Having chosen one of the professional/trade associations from above, make a note of why you might join one of these when you enter the sector.

# Job Roles in the Creative Industries

Having looked at the different sectors available within the media and creative industries, we can now focus on specific jobs within those sectors that might interest you.

## Exercise: Researching Job Roles within the Media and Creative Industries

For this exercise you are invited to research job roles in the media and creative industries. First, have a look at the websites below which list some of the job roles that exist in some of the sectors that make up the media and creative industries:

- Discover Creative Careers – lists job roles including audio production editor, casting director, **director of photography (DoP)**, film marketing assistant, floor runner and lighting designer
- Prospects website – allows you to search for job roles by browsing A to Z or by sector
- ScreenSkills – lists job role profiles under headings such as film and TV drama, **visual effects (VFX)**, games, animation, unscripted TV
- StartinTV – a website listing job roles, explaining what duties are covered by the role and how to get started

Choose the role that most appeals to you. It may be something that you have not heard of before and that arouses your curiosity. Now produce a mini case study of your chosen role. You could investigate the aspects of the role listed below:

- The job description
- The person specifications for the job
- How this role might develop in the future (for example, the future prospects and developments within the industry)

Keep this information as it will be useful at a later date, such as when you are undertaking a career case study in Chapter 4 or sourcing a placement in Chapter 6.

─── **Student Voice** ───────────────────────────────

"Research into specific roles, for example, I began by watching the credits of TV shows, researching roles I had no idea about, then researching specific people in roles that took my interest to investigate how they ended up where they are today."

*– Liv Louis, Freelance Production Runner/Media Production student*

# Conclusion

Hopefully, by now you will have gained a great deal of insight into what the media and creative industries can offer you. This chapter has given you an overview of the media and creative industries sectors, and it has also helped you to identify the types of jobs that are relevant to your degree course.

In the next chapter we will analyse key skills and qualities in order to give you a better idea of what prospective employers are looking for.

## Further Reading

Davies, Rosamund, and Sigthorsson, Gauti (2013) *Introducing the Creative Industries: From Theory to Practice*. London: Sage. This book provides further information on the history, trends, products and markets of the creative industries.

DCMS (2015, January) 'Creative Industries Economic Estimates January 2015 – key findings'. www.gov.uk/government/statistics/creative-industries-economic-estimates-january-2015/creative-industries-economic-estimates-january-2015-key-findings

Gregory, Georgina, Healy, Ros, and Mazierska, Ewa (2007) *Careers in Media and Film: The Essential Guide*. London: Sage. This practical handbook offers encouragement, advice, information and case studies to help students to pursue careers in media and film.

Hesmondhalgh, David (2019) *The Cultural Industries* (4th edition). London: Sage. This book provides a critical exploration of cultural production and consumption.

# 3

# ANALYSING YOUR SKILLS AND QUALITIES

## Identifying What Employers are Looking For

## Introduction

In the previous chapter you gained an insight into the media and creative industries and looked into different job sectors and job roles. We will now delve a bit deeper by looking at the skillsets required for a career in the media and creative industries.

This chapter will:

- look at your personal career preferences
- look at the skills and qualities employers are looking for in graduates
- help you to identify which skills and qualities are applicable to your chosen career area

List of exercises in this chapter:

- Undertaking the career planner and job match tests
- Analysing your personal career preferences
- Exploring the qualities for an entrepreneurial mindset
- Finding out about the skills and qualities required for specific areas
- Undertaking a skills and qualities audit

# Exploring Your Career Preferences

We have previously directed you to the Prospects website as a way of finding careers advice and finding out where media graduates look for work. In this section, the exercises will help you to focus on what would be appropriate for you.

## Exercise: Undertaking the Career Planner and Job Match Tests

For this exercise, take the Prospects 'career planner' test or the 'job match' test, or both. These tests help you to identify what job would suit you by matching your skills, motivations and desires to a career. They also offer some suggested professions and provide information on the jobs it has identified might suit you, detailing what each job entails. It is very important that you sign up to prospects.ac.uk and complete your profile before taking either test to make sure you receive the most accurate suggestions.

Once you have undertaken the test/s you should reflect on what you have discovered about the jobs you have been matched with. Are there any career matches that have taken you by surprise? What skillsets do you feel you need to develop further as a result of this exercise?

# Analysing Personal Career Preferences

Davies and Sigthorsson (2013: 93) suggest that 'level of pay is not what primarily motivates and satisfies workers'; instead, it is the 'creative and cultural benefits that they perceive in the work [that keeps] them in the job'. So, it is worth thinking about whether the specific culture of the creative industries will suit you.

A good place to start is to consider what you want from your career. Bear in mind that your career preferences will change over time, but the focus here is on your thoughts at the moment. In the last chapter we looked at what it is like to work in the media and creative industries. Now you should think in detail about what you want to get out of work, your career and your life in the long run. The exercise below encourages you to analyse what is important to you in your future career.

## Exercise: Analysing Your Personal Career Preferences

The following table encourages you to analyse what is important to you in your future career. Have a go at completing the table by putting 'X' in the relevant columns, using the rating scale of 1 being unsuited to you and 5 being very suited to you.

If your Xs are mostly in the two left columns, then the media and creative industries may not be suited to you. If they are mostly in the middle, you have some interest in this career but may need to consider how to make yourself more suited to the media and creative industries. If your Xs are mostly to the right, then your career preferences are suited to the media and creative industries.

| Career preferences | Explanation | 1 | 2 | 3 | 4 | 5 |
|---|---|---|---|---|---|---|
| Self-employed/freelance | Many roles in the media and creative industries are freelance or self-employed. How much does this suit you? | | | | | |
| Job satisfaction | Jobs in the media and creative industries may be less secure and well paid but tend to offer higher job satisfaction. How important is job satisfaction to you? | | | | | |
| Travel | Some jobs in the media and creative industries will involve a lot of travel. How attractive is this to you? | | | | | |
| Working hours and working patterns (flexible hours, fixed hours, shift work, unsociable hours) | Jobs in the media and creative industries tend to have variable hours and patterns. How happy are you to work with variable work patterns? | | | | | |
| Contract (permanent or temporary) | Many contracts in the media and creative industries will be temporary. Would a series of temporary contracts be agreeable to you? | | | | | |
| Remote (home) working | The media and creative industries are often remote/home based, rather than office based. How much would this way of working suit you? | | | | | |
| Interpersonal aspects of the job | Jobs in the media and creative industries tend to involve a lot of collaborative work. How much would this suit your way of working? | | | | | |
| Autonomy | Control over your own workload is often a feature of jobs in the media and creative industries. How important is autonomy to you? | | | | | |
| Networking | Networking is essential for most jobs in the media and creative industries. How comfortable would you feel in a job that requires a lot of networking? | | | | | |
| Need for presentation skills | Compared to many other industries, the media and creative industries rely heavily on presentation skills. How much does this suit you? | | | | | |

You might want to refer back to this list of career preferences as you learn more about working in the media and creative industries from this book.

─( **Hear from the Expert** )──────────────────────────────

"With remote working, some people can feel disconnected because you don't get those social interactions in. The structure and the day can kind of blend into each other, and you can find yourself sitting at the desk and then realise that you've missed lunch. You haven't got up and got away from your desk and gone for a walk. You've got to be self-motivated. When you're working remotely, you have to make sure that you're ready on time, and you know you're ready to start the day on time. If you've got client calls/meetings, or calls with colleagues, your time keeping is really important. So, you've got to make sure that you have that discipline. It's also important you don't leave anybody waiting for you 'because it's not the same as in the office', where people expect you to be there and it's very visible. So remotely you know you do have to be a self-starter and very self-motivated and keep the professionalism you would have in person when you are on calls."

*– Simon Elliott, Managing Director, Diversity Agency*

## Considering Self-employment, Freelancing and Entrepreneurship

So far, we have focused mainly on jobs and careers where your employer is a large corporation or a **small to medium-sized enterprise (SME)**. Much of the work in the media and creative industries is either freelance (where you work on contracts for one or more employer) or you are self-employed and run your own business. We will revisit self-employment in more detail in Chapter 5, but it is worth mentioning it at this early stage because it is a fact of media and creative industries life.

Dr Sally Caird from the Open University argues that an enterprising person is someone who feels confident in initiating and overseeing projects. She lists the following characteristics that contribute to this mindset (Caird, 1990):

- Achievement – an enterprising person has a high need for achievement in all that they do
- **Autonomy** – an enterprising person likes to be in control, whether in a team or working alone
- **Creativity** – an enterprising person is highly imaginative and innovative in their approach to problem-solving
- Risk-taking – an enterprising person is comfortable with taking risks to pursue their goals
- **Locus of control** – an enterprising person believes that they have control over their own destiny

You may already have demonstrated some of these characteristics in the projects you have undertaken at university. For example, you may tend to be a team leader rather than a follower, or you may like to take risks by striving not to go for easy options, or you may not be shy about standing out from the crowd.

The following exercise will enable you to analyse your entrepreneurial mindset and suitability for this type of work.

## Exercise: Exploring the Qualities for an Entrepreneurial Mindset

Below are Caird's (1990) characteristics for an entrepreneurial mindset and the personal qualities that contribute to these. This exercise will help you to explore the extent to which you have an entrepreneurial mindset and how this will influence your career options and future development.

Look at the qualities listed below for achievement, autonomy, creativity, risk-taking and locus of control. Choose one quality from each of the categories to analyse how they reflect your own mindset. What does this tell you about the extent to which you have an entrepreneurial mindset, and therefore how suited you might be to working for yourself in the future?

### Achievement – an Enterprising Person Has a High Need for Achievement in all that they do

Qualities for achievement:

- an orientation towards the future
- a self-reliance on one's own ability
- an optimistic rather than a pessimistic outlook
- a strong task orientation
- an effective approach to time management
- an orientation towards results, which applies to self and others
- a restlessness, with a strong drive and high energy levels
- a tendency to be opinionated and ready to defend ideas and views
- a determination to ensure objectives are met, even when difficulties arise
- a responsible and persistent approach in the pursuit of aims
- a tendency to be goal-orientated, setting challenging but realistic goals
- a willingness to work long and hard when necessary to complete tasks

### Autonomy – an Enterprising Person Likes to be In Control Whether in a Team or Working Alone

Qualities for autonomy:

- independence, preferring to work alone, especially if they cannot be the leader
- strong self-expression, feeling the need to do what they want to do in their way, rather than work on other people's initiatives
- individualism, being able to stand alone even when pressurised by people and groups
- leadership orientation, preferring to be in charge and disliking taking orders

- unconventional, being prepared to stand out as being different from others
- opinionated, and having to say what they think about issues
- determination, being strong willed and stubborn about their interests

## Creativity – an Enterprising Person is Highly Imaginative and Innovative in their Approach to Problem-solving

Qualities for creativity:

- imaginative, with an inventive or innovative tendency to come up with new ideas
- intuitive, being able to synthesise ideas and knowledge, and make good guesses when necessary
- change-oriented, preferring novelty, change and challenge, with a dislike of being locked into routines
- versatile, being able to draw on personal resources for projects or problem-solving
- curiosity, with an interest in new ideas

## Risk-taking – an Enterprising Person is Comfortable with Taking Risks to Pursue their Goals

Qualities for risk-taking:

- decisive, being able to act on incomplete information and being good at judging when incomplete information is sufficient for taking action
- a self-awareness, with the ability to accurately assess their own capability
- analytical, being good at evaluating the likely benefits against the likely costs of actions
- a tendency to be goal-oriented, setting challenging but attainable goals
- effective with information management, using information to calculate the probability of success

## Locus of Control – an Enterprising Person Believes that they Have Control Over Their Own Destiny

Qualities for locus of control:

- opportunistic, seeking and taking advantage of opportunities
- self-confident, with the belief that they have control over their destiny and make their own luck, rather than being controlled by fate
- **proactive**, taking personal responsibility to navigate the problems that arise to achieve success on their terms
- determined, expressing a strong will and effort to control their life
- self-believing, equating the results achieved with the effort made

# Exploring Entrepreneurial Competencies

Another way to explore your entrepreneurial spirit is to undertake a self-assessment that enables you to understand and articulate your entrepreneurial competence. Go to the YOOP website (yoop.fi/en/) and choose the 'Map your entrepreneurship competence' link on the menu to start your self-assessment. You will be asked a series of yes/no questions and to give an example and justification of your choice of answer. This will result in a PDF document demonstrating your entrepreneurial competence which you can use in many contexts. We will be looking in more detail at this in Chapter 5 where we discuss working for yourself.

---

## Hear from the Expert

"I'd say confidence and humility are important. You've got to be very sure of yourself. There's a need to come across well but also combined with humility as well and being humble. Always being willing to learn from others. It's no good going into a job and coming across as arrogant. You've got to have a very fine balance between self-confidence but also knowing that you can always do better, and you can always learn more from your peers."

*– Eugene Kogut, Videographer*

---

# What Skills and Qualities are Employers Looking For?

We now move on to looking in detail at what employers are looking for in their graduate employees. Most employers are not so concerned with what specific degree you did, but that you have a degree in the first place. They are looking for a wide-ranging list of skills and qualities that are developed on a range of degree courses. Let's examine what it is employers are looking for in graduates.

A report called *The Future of Jobs* by the World Economic Forum (2020) provides detailed information about careers and skills, including data and predictions about the emerging roles/jobs of the future, including some in the media and creative industries. In terms of skills and qualities, the report identifies the following for employees of the future:

1  Analytical thinking and innovation: the ability to take a step back, see the bigger picture and come up with fresh ideas
2  Active learning strategies: the capacity to assimilate and challenge new information
3  Complex problem-solving: finding solutions to new, ill-defined problems in dynamic, real-world settings

4   Critical thinking and analysis: using logic to identify the benefits and drawbacks of different approaches
5   Creativity, originality and initiative: unusual ways of solving problems and stepping up to face new challenges
6   Leadership and social influence: having integrity and authority to lead others towards a collective goal
7   Technology use: the ability to master technology, both current and emerging
8   Technology design and programming: the ability to create and adapt
9   Resilience, stress tolerance and flexibility: handling change without losing positivity and drive
10   Reasoning and ideation: manipulating information and clear thinking

(World Economic Forum, *The Future of Jobs*, 2020: 36)

## Identifying Transferable Skills

As well as developing skills and qualities from the degree course itself, you will also be developing valuable transferable skills through your wider life as a student. By transferable skills, we mean any skills and qualities you are developing that can be applied in your future career.

Various skills and qualities can be developed via extra-curricular activities such as sports and social clubs and societies. If you are living away from home for the first time, you will be developing life skills through living independently. You will be making friends and building social and future career support networks. You will also be getting work experience through any paid work you are doing while at university. These are all things you can capitalise on in the future. It is recommended that you make best use of the resources and expertise available to you while at university because it is highly likely that these may be harder to take advantage of once you have graduated.

---

### Hear from the Expert

"One aspect of the university experience that prepared me for my current role is the opportunity to access the careers service, where we got to go to events with guest speakers and got access to additional work experience. This really allowed me to make contacts and attend additional schemes that would give me my contacts who I now work with."

– *Ebony Pascall, Production Manager, BBC Children's and Education*

---

## Analysing Your Hard/Specialist Skills

So far, we have been considering a broad range of skills and qualities you should be developing during your time at university. Now we are going to focus on **hard skills** and specialist skills and their relevance to the media and creative industries.

This refers to practical and job-specific technical skills, such as IT and digital skills, and specialist technical skills, such as the use of media hardware and specific software. Being proficient in digital editing, for example, is a hard/specialist skill.

A report by Sleeman and Windsor for Nesta, called 'A Closer look at Creatives: Using Job Adverts to Identify the Skill Needs of Creative Talent' (2017), presents lists of the skills required for different areas of the creative and media sector.

For example, in Creating and Design Skills, the hard/specialist skills include:

- graphic design
- concept development
- website production
- photography
- music
- video editing
- retail setting

In Marketing Skills, the hard/specialist skills include:

- social media
- copy writing
- advertising design
- press releases
- newsletters
- e-commerce
- optimisation

Specialist software is also mentioned in these types of job descriptions, some of which you will need to use regularly to remain proficient in them. If you go to Sleeman and Windsor's (2017) report in the further reading for this chapter you will find more comprehensive lists of specialist skills.

## Exercise: Finding out About the Skills and Qualities Required for Specific Areas

In this exercise you are going to look at all of the skills that are required for the specific areas you are interested in pursuing. It requires you to look at 'live' job adverts to see what skills and qualities are listed in the requirements for the job. This will give you an idea of how important it is to be aware of the skills that are needed for certain jobs.

For this exercise, decide on a job sector to analyse and locate an advert for the sort of job you would like to ultimately pursue. Here are some suggested websites for you to look for job adverts, but you might want to look for your own too.

Media, film and television jobs:

- Creative Access (creativeaccess.org.uk) – opportunities in the creative sector
- The Unit List (theunitlist.com) – jobs in broadcast

Radio/audio jobs:

*   Podjobs (podjobs.net) – jobs in podcasting
*   RadioToday (radiotoday.co.uk) – jobs in radio

Advertising, marketing and PR jobs:

*   CampaignJobs (campaignlive.co.uk) – jobs in the media, marketing and creative sectors
*   Marketing Week Jobs (jobs.marketingweek.com) – jobs in the marketing industry

Games industry jobs:

*   ACCESSVFX (accessvfx.org) – diversity/support for the games industry
*   Games Jobs Direct (gamesjobsdirect.com) – jobs in the games industry

Creative sector jobs:

*   If You Could (ifyoucouldjobs.com) – jobs for the creative sector
*   IPG Mediabrands (ipgmediabrands.com) – jobs for the design industry

Publishing jobs:

*   Creative Access (creativeaccess.org.uk) – jobs in the publishing industry

Once you have found a job advert that interests you, do the following:

*   identify as many skills and qualities as possible that are referred to in your chosen job advert
*   identify any mention of specialist software or proficiency in specialist equipment
*   match your own skills and qualities to the job advert you have found
*   identify where you might need additional specialist training

Reflect on what this tells you about the skills and qualities you currently possess and how you might develop them further to become career-ready.

## Hear from the Experts

"Be a nice person. Because the industry is so small, everybody knows everybody! Hopefully, being a good person comes naturally. There's no place for nasty people in this business!"

*– Emma Snow, Journalist, BBC*

"You could be a really talented motion graphic designer, but not have loads of experience, but you've just got a knack for motion, graphic design, so it's more about quality of work, and particularly student's stage. We're not expecting them to know everything. I much prefer someone that I know is going to be reliable or that is going to show up and be enthusiastic over someone that you know knows the different lenses we need to put on the camera and stuff like that. So, it's more about attitude and availability and willingness. We don't expect them to be the finished article if they're just graduating."

*– Ben Newth, Head of Video at a corporate video company*

"So, the big tip here is that it's okay that you don't know. I never dreamt that I'd be where I am now, I'd be doing the things I am. It was about being accepting and being open, being able to communicate well, and just being honest with yourself at times and pushing wherever you can."

*– Stephan Hayward, Managing Director, Framework Design*

"For my role, being proactive is essential. As the industry and news cycle changes so frequently, it's important to be reactive to place your clients at the heart of relevant conversations."

*– Tamara Samuel, Senior Digital PR Executive*

## Exercise: Undertaking a Skills and Qualities Audit

The table below lists a number of areas of skills and qualities that have been taken from a variety of adverts for media and creative jobs. Undertake your own **skills audit** by completing the table to indicate the areas you could further develop and suggest a strategy you might use for developing/improving each of them.

| Skills and qualities | Example of how you have already achieved this | Strategy for gaining or improving this |
|---|---|---|
| Ability to show enthusiasm and positivity, and sustained commitment to a shared purpose | | |
| Leadership and management skills | | |
| Awareness of cultural and social diversity | | |
| Ability to work successfully both within a team and on own initiative | | |
| Ability to show initiative and motivation and to adapt to change | | |
| Research and analytical skills | | |
| Organisational ability and ability to multi-task | | |
| Time management skills | | |
| Adaptability and flexibility | | |
| Ability to work to deadlines and cope with periodic increases in workload | | |
| Communication, negotiation and interpersonal skills | | |
| Dealing with conflict | | |
| Ability to work to a brief and to give and receive feedback | | |

*(Continued)*

| Skills and qualities | Example of how you have already achieved this | Strategy for gaining or improving this |
| --- | --- | --- |
| Project management, problem-solving skills and decision-making skills | | |
| Social media and networking skills | | |
| Written, spoken and presentation skills | | |
| Ability to be innovative and creative | | |
| Commercial and sector awareness | | |
| Resilience and **assertiveness** | | |
| Self-awareness and emotional intelligence | | |

## Hear from the Experts

"Don't shy away from things that are unfamiliar. Test yourself. If there's a project that you can get involved with, or if there's a skill that you're not particularly confident with but you have the chance to develop it further, then don't shy away from it. Embrace the opportunity and try to learn some new skills because it's all part of your ongoing personal development."

*– Tom Walters, Account Director, The Dairy*

"The importance of communication and the importance of making sure that you've got your systems. The real technical skills are taken as read. As you study, you will build up those technical skills, will then get to put them into practice when you go into the working world and with a lot of placements that you do. But actually, the skills that really help are the communication and getting your administration in order."

*– Simon Elliott, Managing Director, Diversity Agency*

"We appreciate that as an intern, you probably won't have much experience. Remember, we're not looking for a full-time member of staff, so we're not expecting you to reel off lots of industry-specific experience. I always want to know what an applicant is interested in and to get to know the person. For me it's as much about the person and the personality as it is about the industry-specific skills. I can get a good feel for somebody very quickly if they're personable and sociable. I want them to talk to me about where they're from, what their interests and hobbies are, what they're studying, how they're finding university life and how their studies are going. It's also good to understand their career passions – so are they interested in digital marketing, or PR, or design? By having answers to these questions, I can understand how the candidate will best slot into the team because that chemistry is vital in a creative space. So, for me, an interview is about the person and their personality, their attitude and their communication skills. Demonstrating strong soft skills and having a warm personality are really important."

*– Tom Walters, Account Director, The Dairy*

"Focus on your communication and interpersonal skills because without those skills, you will not know how to speak to employers from industry in a professional and clear way"

*– Radha Singh, CEO/Creative Director, THE HOUSE OF RADHA*

# Finding Out About Skills Shortages

So far, we have examined skills that employers are looking for in employees. You can also benefit from finding out about skills shortages that exist in the area you plan to work in. This may influence the specific job that you are looking for. Various reports have been published identifying areas of skills shortages. It will be worth investigating these reports further to help you focus on areas where you may want to personally plug the skills gap. Identifying gaps may also make you consider changing the area you want to pursue.

For example, according to the *Sector Insights: Skills and Performance Challenges in the Digital and Creative Sector Report* (UK Commission for Employment and Skills, 2015: 48):

> Historically there has been a tendency to categorise workers within the digi-
> tal and creative sector as either 'creative' or 'technical' or 'management'. This
> has been reinforced by the education system which often forces individuals
> to choose between the arts or sciences. Those focusing on the former may not
> develop technical skills, while those in the latter path may not be given the
> chance to develop their creativity.

However, the *Annual ScreenSkills Assessment: August 2019* reports that 'the main reasons for skills gaps in the sector are that recruits are new to the role (65%) or that the employee's training is only partially complete (60%), both suggesting that, for the most part, training is taking place and that skills gaps are largely transient in nature' (Work Foundation, 2019: 43).

Clearly, employees (and therefore graduates) in the sector need up-to-date technical skills as well as creativity, and these technical skills need to be monitored, and staff re-trained, to keep up with the latest advances.

The Creative Industries Federation report, *Creative Industries Jobs – Risks and Opportunities* (n.d.), states that the creative industries are worth £87.4 billion to the economy and that these industries are creating jobs four times as quickly as the wider economy. However, there are threats to its continued success due to skills shortages. One of the problems caused by skills shortages is that there is 'a lack of awareness about the careers that the sector has to offer' (Creative Industries Federation, n.d.).

The report lists many of the sectors we have already outlined in this book, including advertising and media, broadcasting, design, fashion, film, music, and photography. It highlights, however, that the major skills gaps are in those jobs that require a mix of creative and technical skills. Graduates who have a good level of technical prowess but who can think analytically and creatively, and have a strong awareness of cultural values, are the types of employees needed to fill these skills gaps.

As well as searching for relevant reports, such as those listed above, to help you research skills gaps and skills shortages, you can also try searching online for 'skills employers want in the media and creative industries' or 'skills shortages in the media and creative industries', or swap this with the name of the specific industry sector you are interested in.

# Training and Continuing Professional Development

In this chapter we have been discussing the work skills and qualities that employers are looking for. It is certainly not the case that employers will expect you to come to them with a full set of skills and competencies. In most organisations, you will be encouraged or required to undertake **continuing professional development (CPD)**.

A number of organisations provide masterclasses and training courses which are available to professionals working within the industry and for people working for themselves. Some examples that you can investigate are:

* The National Film and Television School (NFTS.co.uk) – offers short courses in film and TV
* ScreenSkills (screenskills.com) – the section on developing your career offers training courses, masterclasses and mentoring for people working in the screen industries
* The Digital Garage (learndigital.withgoogle.com) – offers training for the digital workplace
* LinkedIn Learning (linkedin.com/learning) – offers training in many different areas to support the development of creative career-related skills

You may benefit from looking at such opportunities for skills development while still at university where it will normally be free to access.

# Conclusion

In this chapter we have analysed some of the skills and qualities required for the media and creative industries. We have encouraged you to do research into skills gaps in your chosen careers sector, and to identify which skills are applicable to your chosen career. The exercises you have conducted throughout this chapter should not only give you an insight into skills and qualities employers are looking for, but should also help to give you confidence in your future planning and search for work.

In the next chapter we will consider potential career areas and you will conduct a career case study.

## Further Reading

The following reading will be useful for further investigation into skills and qualities required for working in the media and creative industries, and the skills and qualities employers are looking for.

Caird, Sally (1990) 'What does it mean to be enterprising?' British Journal of
    Management, 1(3), 137–145. http://dx.doi.org/10.1111/j.1467-8551.1990.tb00002.x
Creative Industries Federation (n.d.) *Creative Industries Jobs – Risks and Opportunities*.
    London: CFI. Available at: www.creativeindustriesfederation.com/sites/default/
    files/2017-09/Creative%20industries%20workforce.pdf
Dass, Matthew, Goodwin, Andrew, Wood, Melissa, and Luanaigh, Aoife (2015) *Sector
    Insights: Skills Challenges in the Digital and Creative Sector*. UK Commission for
    Employment Skills report. London: UK Commission for Employment Skills.
Sleeman, Cath, and Windsor, George (2017, April 18) 'A closer look at creatives: Using
    job adverts to identify the skill needs of creative talent'. *Nesta* [website]. www.nesta.
    org.uk/blog/a-closer-look-at-creatives/
UK Commission for Employment and Skills (2015, June 9) *Sector Insights:
    Skills and Performance Challenges in the Digital and Creative Sector Report*.
    London: UKCES. Available at: www.gov.uk/government/publications/
    sector-insights-skills-and-performance-challenges-in-the-digital-and-creative-sector
Work Foundation (2019, August 16) *Annual ScreenSkills Assessment: August 2019*.
    London and Lancaster: Work Foundation. Available at: www.screenskills.com/
    media/2853/2019-08-16-annual-screenskills-assessment.pdf
World Economic Forum (2020, October 20) *The Future of Jobs Report 2020*. Cologny,
    Switzerland: World Economic Forum. Available at: www.weforum.org/reports/
    the-future-of-jobs-report-2020/

We also recommend:
Davies, Rosamund, and Sigthorsson, Gauti (2013) *Introducing the Creative Industries:
    From Theory to Practice*. London: Sage. This book provides further information on the
    history, trends, products and markets of the creative industries.

# 4

# EXPLORING POTENTIAL CAREER AREAS

## Researching Career Case Studies

## Introduction

In Chapter 2 we directed you to look at some online profiles in a range of different jobs and career areas. In this chapter you get the chance to conduct your own **career case study**. We will assist you in performing a research exercise where you look in detail at a number of aspects of a job/career area you think you might be interested in. You will make contact with and interview an employee in the media and creative industries in order to learn from their experience. We include a guide to formulating questions and include examples of the types of questions you could ask.

The aims and outcomes of this chapter are:

- to decide on a job/career area of focus for your career case study
- to research the job/career you have chosen to focus your case study on
- to learn more about the job/career of interest

List of exercises in this chapter:

- Performing a mock job hunt
- Aligning your job choices with your personal values and career aspirations
- Conducting a career case study

We start this chapter with an exercise that gives you the opportunity to engage in a mock job hunt. This will be good preparation for deciding on what you would like to focus your placement and work experience on.

## Exercise: Performing a Mock Job Hunt

You should research your own sources for this mock job hunt, but there are some links below to get you started in searching for jobs in the UK media and creative industries. They are loosely grouped into the sectors that we have focused on so far in this book.

For this exercise, you are required to look for adverts for the sort of job that you may enter on graduation (and beyond). Follow the instructions below.

Select the sites from the list that follows which link most closely to your career (and placement) aspirations and undertake a mock job hunt. You should aim to find job adverts for three jobs which satisfy the following conditions:

- the first job advert should be suitable for a graduate: in other words, an entry-level job that you might apply for if you were graduating tomorrow
- the second should be a job which you would like to have within five years of graduating
- the third job advert should be for one that would be your ultimate job ambition (in an ideal world) at the height of your career

Having found the three job adverts, reflect on how this has influenced your decisions about what you might want to do for a future job/career. Identify anything that has surprised you in your research.

## Links for Your Mock Job Hunt

You can start your research with the Mediabeans website (mediabeans.io), which lists UK and remote jobs in writing, journalism, social media and communications. You can then go to some of the websites below which have been categorised under broad sector headings.

## Media, Film and Television Jobs

- 4 Careers (careers.channel4.com) – the Channel 4 jobs website, which includes pages on apprenticeships and training schemes
- BBC Careers (careerssearch.bbc.co.uk) – the BBC careers website
- The Call Sheet (thecallsheet.co.uk) – film and TV jobs and crew lists
- Creative Access (creativeaccess.org.uk) – opportunities in the creative sector for people from diverse backgrounds
- The Freelance Video Collective (freelancevideocollective.com) – a jobs board for freelance media jobs
- ITV Jobs (itvjobs.com) – the ITV careers website
- Mandy (mandy.com) – a site for film, TV and production jobs
- Media Parents (mediaparents.co.uk) – a support site for people who work in the industry and which also advertises jobs
- My First Job in Film (myfirstjobinfilm.com) – jobs in the film industry
- Shooting People (shootingpeople.org) – independent film makers network and jobs site

- Sky Careers (careerssky.com) – a careers website for Sky TV
- Startin TV (startintv.com) – a site for accessing the TV industry
- The Talent Manager (thetalentmanager.com) – freelance jobs in the creative sector
- TV Watercooler (tvwatercooler.org) – a database of jobs in media
- The Unit List (theunitlist.com) – jobs in broadcasting

## Hear from the Expert

"Usually, for industry updates or vacancies I use the recruitment and networking plat-form The Talent Manager – it's similar to LinkedIn but caters for the TV and film industry. Surprisingly, there's also a wealth of private Facebook groups for people working in the industry and this is hugely popular and something many of my fellow colleagues take advantage of. There's typically a lot of information and updates posted and many job offerings. Early on in my career, the majority of entry-level jobs I secured were through these Facebook groups and, depending on where you live, there is also more localised versions."

*– Marco Murru, Storyliner, Warner Bros UK*

## Radio/Audio Jobs

- Podjobs (podjobs.net) – jobs in podcasting
- RadioToday (radiotoday.co.uk) – jobs in radio

## Advertising, Marketing and PR Jobs

- Campaign Jobs (campaignlive.co.uk) – a site for jobs in the media, marketing and creative sectors
- Marketing Week Jobs (jobs.marketingweek.com) – a professional site for jobs in the marketing industry

## Jobs in the Games Industry

- Games Jobs Direct (gamesjobsdirect.com) – a jobs site for the games industry

## Creative Sector Jobs

- If You Could (ifyoucouldjobs.com) – a jobs site for the creative sector

## Third Sector Jobs

- Third sector jobs (jobs.thirdsector.co.uk) – a jobs site that includes media and creative jobs in the third sector (voluntary, charity and not-for-profit organisations)

Now that you have found examples of three jobs that you are interested in and considered them for three stages in your career journey, choose *one* of these jobs to focus on for your career case study. The purpose of this exercise is to narrow down your career area from the broad 'media and creative' into a more focused description, such as 'social media manager', 'casting director', 'advertising account executive', or 'podcast producer', for instance.

Thinking back to Chapter 1, where we considered your personal values and preferences for shaping your career options, let us now think about how you can align your choice of jobs with these values. This requires you to research and reflect on how happy you will feel working for a chosen company.

## Exercise: Aligning Your Job Choices with Your Personal Values and Career Aspirations

This exercise will consider how you might make job choices based on your personal values. Focusing on the chosen job, you can now take into account aspects such as the employer's commitment to equality, diversity and inclusion (EDI), their commitment to sustainability and their level of **corporate social responsibility (CSR)**.

You can find information about the company's policies and practices in the following places:

- the job advert for the job you are researching
- the company's website and their social media
- the company's reports and **Human Resources (HR)** policy
- the company's presence in the trade and other press

To help you with this exercise, we are offering an example based on employer policies of inclusion for LGBTQ+ employees based on research by Turton on the Adzuna (adzuna.co.uk) website. They offer some tips for you to check if an employer is LGBTQ+ inclusive. You can use the same principles when researching your particular personal values and social and cultural context.

- Look for a statement of support – Does the employer encourage applications from diverse candidates in a short, written statement or do they have diversity and inclusion statements on their website or career pages?
- Check their social media profiles – Does the employer's LinkedIn, Facebook, Twitter/X and Instagram mention Pride events? Is the company organising their own Pride celebration or flying the Rainbow flag during Pride month?
- Ask if they have a LGBTQ+ champion – Is there a dedicated member of the company's team who can answer questions about company culture and inclusivity?
- Scrutinise HR policy – Does the company use gender-neutral language in their policies, such as 'partner', 'parent', 'spouse' instead of 'wife' or 'father'? Do they have policies such as 'adoption leave' as well as 'paternity' and 'maternity' leave?

(Turton, adzuna.co.uk, 2021)

Once you have gathered as much information as you can find, reflect on how happy you would feel to be part of the company you have researched.

# Learning from Case Studies of Job Roles in the Media and Creative Industries

Before you embark on your career case study interview it will be useful to investigate profiles of, and interviews with, people in specific jobs that are available online. This will give you a flavour of the sorts of roles that might be available to you and how a case study might look.

- Go to the Job Profiles section of the ScreenSkills website (screenskills.com). Find your chosen sector, and then a job role profile within that sector
- Go to the icould website (icould.com) and find the 'explore careers' tab. Then search for 'job type'. Select the sector that you are interested in
- Go to the BBC Bitesize website (bbc.co.uk/bbcbitesize) and find 'job profiles'. Then choose between TV and film, radio, journalism, performing arts, and games and design

## Exercise: Conducting Your Career Case Study

An important aspect of the career case study is to learn directly from a mentor who is employed in the career you are researching. You will conduct an interview to gain this information. Start by searching for a mentor to interview. A mentor is somebody who can support and advise you about your career journey based on their own experience. This exercise will also help you to build your networks further.

It is worth spending some time on this exercise as the more effort you put into it, the more valuable the outcome will be. You will be receiving information directly from someone who already has experience of working in your chosen career area.

We will guide you through the process step by step, by briefing you on the exercise, then recommending how you go through the process of contacting someone, then writing/choosing some interview questions, and finally conducting the interview.

### Where to Find Your Interviewee/s

You can find your interviewee/s from a variety of sources. The following suggestions are very useful:

- Search through LinkedIn for people (and companies) working in the area you are interested in. Especially useful for the interview for the case study is the LinkedIn Alumni tool that you used in Chapter 1. You will be surprised how many people on LinkedIn will be willing to help you with an interview

- Think about your friends and family and your wider networks, and if there is anyone who might be able to provide you with an interview about your chosen career area
- Consider your peers, as they may have friends and relatives who are working in the area you are keen on
- Contact any previous placement/work experience provider you have worked with as a potential mentor
- Don't be afraid to make speculative contacts with people you feel may be able to help you

## How to Conduct Your Interview

You can conduct your interview in any way you like, perhaps using one of the following:

- video interview (via Teams, Zoom or similar)
- an interview conducted over email, via LinkedIn or other social media
- a survey questionnaire (using Microsoft Forms, for example)
- an audio interview over the phone
- a face-to-face interview

Make sure you appreciate which form would be the most suitable for your interviewee, maybe giving them a choice. Some might prefer talking on camera to having to write up answers to your questions in an email. It would be a good idea to record the interview in order to be able to transcribe it. It is important that you gain written consent from your interviewee prior to recording them so you have evidence of their agreement to be interviewed.

When conducting primary research, it is a good idea to keep a note of how you carried out the research and to reflect on the success of the methodology. For example, if you conducted the research via survey or email, was it as satisfactory as it would have been if you had spoken to the person on the phone or via a video call? The purpose of making notes is mainly to keep a record of the methods you used in case you wish to carry out similar research in the future – in which case you can improve on the methods, if needed.

Your interview should open with the following information:

- the name of the interviewee
- their job title
- where their job is located
- who they work for
- where you found them
- whether they went to university, where they studied and what degree course they took
- any other educational path they have taken

You should include evidence that the interviewee has given consent to be interviewed and consent to be recorded (if appropriate).

You are advised to choose a selection from the questions in the following exercise. Try not to bombard your interviewee with too many questions on a diverse range of topics. Once you have established a relationship, you can always go back and ask further questions. Alternatively, you can share your questions between several interviewees.

The information you will be trying to elicit from the interview is:

- the job description
- the person specifications
- the skills required
- experience required
- qualifications required
- how university might prepare you for a job
- where the jobs are located
- applying for and interviewing for a job
- the promotion, career structure and future prospects of a job
- the salary levels
- typical 'work culture' of the career area in focus
- the make-up of the industry and future likely developments
- networking opportunities
- other more general questions

This career case study exercise is structured into 14 sections. Within each of these sections we provide suggested questions to aid you with your research.

## 1. Research the Job Description

Job adverts always start with a job description (JD), which describes the role and responsibilities expected of the applicant for the job, and a list of the sorts of duties that will be carried out.

From the examples of the live advert that you have found in the mock job hunt above, look at the job descriptions and identify the main duties and responsibilities of the job in question. Add this content to your career case study to provide some background context.

Next, ask your mentor some questions about the job description for their job. You could ask the following sorts of questions:

- Can you give a summary of the job description for your job?
- What is a typical day or week for you?
- How much responsibility do you get given in your job?

Having received the answers, consider what you have found out about the job description and whether this job still appeals to you. You can now add this to your case study.

## 2. Research the Person Specifications for the Job

A **person specification** or 'person spec' is a list of selection criteria for the ideal candidate for a job. It includes the skills, qualities, attributes, experience and qualifications which are usually categorised as 'essential' or 'desirable'.

From the live adverts you have found, look for some examples of person specifications for the job and add this to your case study.

Next, ask your mentor some questions about the person specifications for their job. You could ask the following sorts of questions:

- How would you expect your employer to describe the essential person specifications for your job?
- How would you expect your employer to describe the desirable person specifications for your job?
- Would you consider that there are any specific personal qualities and personality characteristics that are essential for your role?

In your case study, consider how you match with the 'essential' and 'desirable' attributes for the job. Are there any areas that you feel you might want to develop further?

## 3. Research the Skills Required for the Job

In Chapter 3 we helped you to identify which skills are applicable to your chosen career area. This included considering the skills that employers are looking for.

Ask your mentor some questions about the skills required for their job. You could ask them the following sorts of questions:

- What do you think are the top three skills that your employer requires of you in your job?
- Can you give three transferable skills that are useful/necessary in your job?
- Can you give three specialist skills (for example, use of equipment or software) that are useful/necessary in your job?

How do your mentor's answers relate to your own skillset and your future career aspirations? What skills areas do you plan to enhance further as a result of your findings?

## 4. Experience Required for the Job

Most job adverts will outline the type of experience that the employer would like the ideal candidate to have. This includes experience from jobs, placements and other work experience.

Ask your mentor some questions about the experience required for their job. You could ask them the following sorts of questions:

- Can you detail the work experience and placements you undertook at university that contributed to your relevant experience for your current job?
- How has any other type of experience (volunteering, hobbies and interests, and part-time jobs) been useful for your job?
- Can you detail the relevant experience you gained through other jobs since graduating?

As a result of your findings, what similar types of experience have you gained that you can add to your list, and are there any other areas of experience that you need to acquire while on your degree course?

## 5. Qualifications Required for the Job

Job adverts will often mention the qualifications that are required, but in a general rather than a specific way. For example, it may suggest a 'good' degree in any subject area. Some jobs, however, may require professional, accredited qualifications.

Ask your mentor some questions about the qualifications required for their job. You could ask them the following sorts of questions:

- What qualifications did you need for your job?
- Do you have or do you require any additional or professional accredited qualifications for your job?
- Are you required to undertake any continuing professional development (CPD) to enhance your qualifications?

What do your findings tell you about the qualifications you already have and what areas you might want to work on further?

## 6. How University Might Prepare You for the Job

You don't necessarily require a degree in media to go into the media and creative industries, but it can help. What is important is how your degree has prepared you for the career area you are interested in. Employers are also interested in what you gain from your wider university experience.

If your mentor went to university, ask them some questions about how it prepared them for their job. You could ask them the following sorts of questions:

- How important was your degree and the degree result to your current job?
- What were the main aspects of subject knowledge and practical skills you learned through your degree course that you now use in your job?
- Can you give one aspect of the wider university experience that helped prepare you for your current job?

Follow this up in your case study by thinking about what you are currently doing at university that could feed usefully into your future career.

## 7. Where the Jobs are Located

Jobs in the media and creative industries tend to be clustered in particular parts of the country or in specific parts of towns and cities (such as creative and cultural quarters). Some jobs may also be located in other parts of the world.

Ask your mentor some questions about where their job is located. You could ask them the following sorts of questions:

- Where is your job located (in the world/country/town or city)?
- How has the location of your job influenced your career path?
- What advice do you have about the importance of job location for someone in their early career?

Having received the answers and recorded them in your case study, consider how important location is to your future career planning. Would you be prepared to relocate to pursue your career goal?

### Hear from the Expert

"My hometown is situated just on the outskirts of Manchester, a huge hub for the television industry. I've been fortunate to have a lot of jobs in the area, but I've also had long-term jobs in both Liverpool and Leeds. Despite these being a considerable commute from my hometown, I've been more than happy to do so. With the Covid-19 pandemic there has been a lot more flexibility with working from home. Unfortunately, as I work in scripted TV, the majority of these jobs are situated in London, so this is something to consider for the long term and it could be likely that I may need to move location to continue furthering my career."

*– Marco Murru, Storyliner, Warner Bros UK*

## 8. Applying for and Interviewing for Your Job

Jobs in the media and creative industries may not always be advertised through conventional channels. Some may be found through word of mouth, others through specific websites, social media channels and trade publications. Therefore, it is important for you to know where to look for opportunities.

Ask your mentor some questions about where to find jobs and where their type of work is advertised. You could ask them the following sorts of questions:

- Where and how did you find your job?
- What was the application process for your job (for example, CV, covering letter, application form, informal phone call, assessment centre, practical task test, presentation, portfolio, **showreel**, or a mixture of the above)?

- What sort of interview did you have to do for your job, how did it go and can you remember any of the questions you were asked?

In your case study, record anything you found surprising in the answers to your questions. How might this information influence your approach to job hunting?

## 9. The Promotion, Career Structure and Future Prospects of the Job

It may be interesting to find out from your mentor what the future holds for the job they are in as a way of thinking about your own potential career path. The following questions will help to give you an insight here:

- What do you think are the likely developments in your career area that might impact in future?
- What are the prospects for career progression?
- What ways would you go about gaining a promotion and working up the career ladder?

Make a note in your case study of how the answers to your questions might shape your future career plan. For example, knowing about the promotion structure of a job could give you a sense of where your path may lead after graduation.

## 10. The Salary Levels

For this set of questions, you should avoid asking direct, personal questions about the mentor's pay. However, it would be useful for you to find out information about typical rates of pay, and how to value your own skills and experience that you have to offer. The following questions will help you:

- What is the typical starting salary for people in your line of work?
- What is the future earning potential of your job?
- If you are self-employed, how do you decide what rate you should charge your clients?

What do the answers tell you about how important salary levels are to you? Would you be willing to start at a relatively low level of pay and build your way up?

## 11. The Typical 'Work Culture' of the Career Area in Focus

For this section you should consider the work culture of the career area/job you are interested in. For example, is it a 9 to 5 office-based job? Is it a portfolio career with jobs spread across the country/world, or outside conventional office hours? You may also consider the sorts of people you will be working with, the hierarchical structure of the organisation, and the social aspects of the job, including achieving a **work–life balance**.

Ask your mentor some questions about their work culture. You could ask them the following sorts of questions:

- Can you describe the work culture of your job? (You may want to give some pointers here, such as working hours, management and organisational structure)
- How do you achieve a reasonable work–life balance?
- How important are the interpersonal aspects of your work, such as teamwork and communication?

Use the information gained here to think about the type of work culture that would suit you best and add this to your case study.

## 12. The Make-up of the Industry and Future Likely Developments

In Chapter 3 we briefly mentioned finding out about the future developments of the media and creative industries and the future skills that will be needed. You could also find some of this information out by asking your mentor the following questions:

- In the next five years, where do you see the industry you work in, and how do you think you will fit into this?
- How do you stay up to date with the latest information, opportunities and future developments in your job/industry?
- Do you access any trade publications or websites to keep abreast of the latest developments in your industry and if so, which ones do you consult?

Use whatever information you have found here to think about how you may situate yourself in jobs that don't yet exist. How will you research the future of the sector you are interested in?

---

### Hear from the Expert

"I believe the success of streaming platforms will continue to impact the television industry on a huge scale. As live television viewers continue to decline, streaming sub-scribers are growing. However, this could be considered as a catch-22. As more companies and streamers are competing, there are more shows being made, allowing more roles within the industry to be filled."

*– Marco Murru, Storyliner, Warner Bros UK*

---

## 13. Networking Opportunities

In whatever job role you find yourself, **networking** is of paramount importance. Every sector has a number of ways of supporting networking, for example through social media, the trade press, professional associations, trade fairs, and through the job itself. Ask your mentor about networking opportunities in their job/career area with the following questions:

- What advice do you have on how to go about networking in your industry?
- How much networking do you do in your daily job, how important is it and what form does it take?
- Do you belong to a union or professional association? If so, what is it and what benefits does it bring?

You could follow this up by investigating any of the networking opportunities your mentor has mentioned, and joining or linking to any that include student membership. Use this to make a plan about how you will approach networking in the future.

## Hear from the Experts

"There is power of networking and real value in meeting everyone – talking to as many people as you can. I was absolutely terrified of networking at university. It scared the life out of me. All I could think [was] that it was just going to be confusing business-speak with a huge nametag. But, five years after graduating you realise it's not the case. Although you still have to wear nametags sometimes."

*– Shauna Wilkinson, Creative, Ginger Root*

"You've got to get your foot in the door and then work your way up from the bottom. Meet industry people and get as much advice as you possibly can and create a contacts book. When you're young, you don't really know what you're doing, so it's important to have a mentor who can guide you. I've learnt some really valuable lessons and I've had some amazing mentors as well. I still keep in contact with them now."

"Having a list of contacts, even if you just write them down or have them in your phone, is really useful. A lot of it is about forming connections and just keeping in touch and being like 'hey, I'm in London, fancy grabbing a coffee?' and things like that."

*– Emma Snow, Journalist, BBC*

## 14. Other More General Questions

You will no doubt have other questions you would like to ask your mentor in the career case study interview. Here are some suggestions of the sorts of things you might like to ask them:

- Are there any additional tips and hints you have for current graduates looking for a role in your employment area?
- What 'do's' and 'don'ts' do you have for graduates looking to join your industry?
- Is there anything you would do differently in your career if you were starting again?

# Reflecting on What You Have Learned from Your Career Case Study Research

As with all work that you carry out, it is important to reflect on what you have learned from the interview. You can write up your reflections and add them to the end of the case study you have created. You should reflect on the following:

- the benefits of working in the sector you are interested in
- the main skills needed for the job you are interested in and how you will develop these skills further
- how you feel you would fit into the work culture
- whether the career area is what you imagined it to be like
- how you might get into the sector
- whether the interview has highlighted any alternative routes or career areas you might look into

# Conclusion

Having conducted the secondary research (the mock job hunt) and primary research (the interview with a mentor) following the guidance in this chapter, you should have gained a more in-depth insight into the career area that you are interested in. This may also influence any placements that you look for, as well as the types of work you pursue after graduation.

It is possible that during your primary research you may have interviewed a freelancer or someone who has experienced some form of self-employment. This style of work is very common in the media and creative industries, and it is what we are going to look at in the next chapter.

## Further Reading

Culver, Sherri Hop, and Seguin, James (2018) *Media Career Guide: Preparing for Jobs in the 21st Century*. Boston, MA and New York: Bedford Books. This book provides a directory of media jobs as well as help in researching companies, applying for jobs, and advice on displaying appropriate behaviour in the workplace.

Turton, Tora (2021). *Adzuna* [Blog]. https://www.adzuna.co.uk/blog/the-most-inclusive-lgbtq-cities-regions-sectors/ Adzuna is a useful site for finding out about labour market information. The article cited in this chapter is focused on the most LGBTQ+ inclusive cities, regions and sectors and how to check if an employer is LGBTQ+ inclusive. You can also use the site to discover a wide range of other aspects of labour market information, such as statistics about pay gaps, articles about inclusivity in the workplace and blogs about different aspects of work culture.

The following books will help with research into specific career areas:

Davies, Gill, and Balkwill, Richard (2011) *The Professional's Guide to Publishing: A Practical Introduction to Working in the Publishing Industry*. London: Kogan Page.

Gallagher, Matt (2016) *Breaking into UK Film and Television Drama for New Entrants and Graduates*. Scotts Valley, CA: CreateSpace Independent Publishing Platform.

Hatschek, Keith (2014) *How to Get a Job in the Music Industry*. Boston, MA: Berklee Press.

Watson, Warren (2019) *Surviving Journalism: Fireproofing a Career in the Fourth Estate*. Portland, OR: Marion Street Press.

# 5

# WORKING FOR YOURSELF

## Considering Entrepreneurship, Freelancing and Self-employment

## Introduction

In the previous chapter we explored potential career areas by researching career case studies. In this chapter we consider the option of working for yourself. We look carefully at the different definitions of enterprise, entrepreneurship, self-employment, and free-lancing. Each is different and so it is important to clearly define all terms. We will also give examples of this type of work.

The aims and outcomes of this chapter are:

- to introduce you to definitions of freelancing, enterprise and entrepreneurship, and self-employment
- to help you consider the pros and cons of working for yourself
- to help you identify skills that you are already developing for this career path and the new ones you may need

List of exercises in this chapter:

- Would working for myself suit me?
- Matching skills and qualities developed at university with skills needed for working for yourself

In Chapter 3 we asked you briefly to consider self-employment, freelancing or entre-preneurship as a career option, and you engaged in an exercise which examined the entrepreneurial mindset. This chapter is important, regardless of your initial assessment of whether you would be suited to working for yourself. At some stages in your career, you may not have a choice; you are entering an industry that has certain sectors that are increasingly reliant on freelancers. Alison Grade identifies that 'approximately 28% of the total screen industries workforce (excluding games) are estimated to be self-employed. However, in film and TV production 50% of workers are freelance' (Grade, 2020: 3). This chapter will highlight the skills and knowledge that you may need to rely on if you find yourself in the self-employment market.

# Definitions of Freelancing, Enterprise and Entrepreneurship, and Self-employment

The terms freelancing, enterprise and entrepreneurship, and self-employment refer to working for yourself, but there are significant differences between these terms that it is useful to be aware of.

## Freelancing

- **Freelancing** is a form of self-employment in which the freelancer has a flexible work routine: pitches to clients for project-based contracts
- advertises and markets their services
- usually works from home
- is responsible for supplying their own up-to-date specialist equipment
- usually organises their own accounting and business administration and management

Davies and Sigthorsson (2013: 45) suggest that 'small-to-medium-sized enterprises (SMEs) very often contract freelancers, rather than employing full-time staff because, in a project-based industry, it allows them more staffing flexibility'. They also highlight that freelancers:

- have short-term relationships with clients rather than long-term contracts with employers
- may receive hourly, weekly, or monthly wages, or a flat fee for each project
- may supply their services or products direct to the public, instead of contracting with a company

(Davies and Sigthorsson, 2013: 45)

## Enterprise and Entrepreneurship

Enterprise and entrepreneurship are often mentioned together but there are slight differences in how they can be defined. An example of enterprise is someone taking an initiative to start a new business, whereas entrepreneurship involves a greater degree of risk-taking. Davies and Sigthorsson (2013: 52) argue that entrepreneurship is 'strongly associated with creativity, problem-solving and having an eye for spotting gaps in the market'. Rook (2019: 266) describes 'entrepreneurship' as 'the process of launching a risky new venture that could lead to either a profit or a loss' and differentiates this from being enterprising, which he describes as being able to 'proactively solve problems and find opportunities'. Smith (2023: n.p.) defines an entrepreneur as 'a person who devises, sets up and runs a new business or businesses' and says that typically they:

- devise untested ideas
- make high-risk decisions
- delegate management to experts
- aim to generate buyer interest in their business

Your university is likely to have a centre for enterprise. It is worth investigating it while you are at university to see how you can be supported in working for yourself if this is a path you want to pursue.

## Self-employment

Both freelancing and enterprise and entrepreneurship involve various levels of self-employment. If you are a freelancer you may choose to set up as a small business selling your services, whereas an entrepreneur may establish a unique new enterprise as a business.

Self-employment involves starting a business where you are responsible for:

- business planning
- advertising and marketing of services
- networking
- contracting and briefing workers/freelancers
- general administration, such as workload planning and setting deadlines
- record keeping, such as expenses, income, receipts and bank statements
- employing an accountant to do book-keeping and tax returns
- invoicing and chasing payments
- organising your own pension plan and making regular pension contributions
- paying income tax (registering with His Majesty's Revenue and Customs (HMRC)), paying National Insurance contributions and registering for and paying VAT (Value Added Tax)
- arranging a number of different insurances (public liability insurance, professional indemnity insurance, contents insurance, business interruption insurance, sickness and income protection insurance)

You will also need to pay close attention to typical rates to charge your clients, which is one of the less straightforward aspects of being self-employed.

---

## Hear from the Expert

"First learn what the basic rate is. Turn to seniors who have been in the business. There are WhatsApp groups, Facebook groups where you can find these people. Or if you end up as a runner someplace, you have a wealth of information at your fingertips. Now you know the threshold you can't go below, decide how much you think you should earn in a year, divide that by the amount of days you want to work and add a percentage on top for taxes, refreshing equipment, healthcare, etc.

And don't be afraid to put your foot down. If the client can't afford your rate, unless there is some wonderful reason or an experience you're going to gain from it, it's not worth your time."

*– Adrian Abbot, self-employed director, producer and editor*

---

# What is it Like to Work for Yourself?

Much of the work in the media and creative industries is project-based rather than long-term and permanent. One of the bonuses of this is that your career doesn't feel repetitive, and you can potentially work on a variety of different projects and meet new people.

---

## Hear from the Expert

"By being consistently motivated to create my own work and develop my own style, I have carved out a niche for myself and have returning clients who come to me for my work because they have seen the things I make for myself and want that for themselves and their brand. Working within the confines of other people's vision and being a cog in their machine is boring and creatively unfulfilling, and no amount of money solves those issues."

*– Adrian Abbott, self-employed director, producer and editor*

---

However, being self-employed (as a freelancer or entrepreneur) comes with extra responsibilities, as Alison Grade states on the ScreenSkills website:

[F]or a freelancer, there is extra work to do over and above your day job; you've got to manage your finances on an irregular income plus you've got to market and sell yourself to find work. It's likely that you will have to complete a tax return to finalise your taxes. … You are also expected to have the equipment you need to do your work. (Grade, 2020: 2)

Although it can be exciting to have independence and source your own work, it can also be stressful and unpredictable. Periods of unemployment might be followed by periods where you have too many offers of work, meaning you have to turn jobs down. You will then wonder if these clients/employers will ask you to work with them again. What if you become ill or get injured and have to take a long time off work? You will need health insurance to cover this. You will also need to set up your own pension plan.

# Benefits and Disadvantages of Working for Yourself

The Prospects website (prospects.ac.uk) provides a useful glimpse into freelancing and self-employment, and their advice is worth considering if you think this might be the route for you. It emphasises that going self-employed and becoming your own boss requires a lot of hard work, but also lists several bonus points, including:

- you have creative freedom and are in charge of the decision-making
- your independence means you can set your own hours
- you can work from home, avoiding office politics and a daily commute
- your earning potential can be higher because you can take on more work when you want to
- you will have the opportunity to work on a range of projects with a number of clients, adding variety to your work

Conversely, the recruitment company Reed (reed.co.uk) identifies the following potential disadvantages of working for yourself:

- no employee benefits (for example, sick pay and holiday pay)
- unpredictable income
- potentially long working hours
- increased responsibility and pressure
- more paperwork (for example, tax returns and accounts)

If you are planning on going into the media and creative industries, you should consider the idea of self-employment and freelancing as an option. It might not necessarily be your number one plan, but you may find that at some stage in your career you will be doing some freelance work in order to progress.

## Hear from the Experts

"One of the biggest advantages about being self-employed is that you're able to be in charge of the direction of the company and all the decisions that are made within that. You have complete ownership. Many people will be attracted to the monetary side of owning a company, but when you find something that you truly enjoy doing, it no longer becomes about the money. That's one of the greatest things about being a freelancer, or business owner, you have the freedom to work on something that becomes a passion rather than a chore."

*– Frederick Bravey, Executive Director of a technology company*

"One of the benefits of being self-employed from my point of view is that you have control of your own time. So, if you have the capacity you can have as much work on as time will allow and you can choose the type of work that you want to do as well."

*– Patricia Francis, filmmaker*

"One of the biggest disadvantages you have to understand when you start a company or you go into freelancing is you're going to need to give up your social life and your social life is most certainly an area that is going to be impacted the most. You're never going to grow your company if you are constantly procrastinating and wasting time that isn't in your company's best interest. You have to dedicate a lot of your time to your work but once you start seeing your accomplishments you will look back and realize why didn't I start this sooner?"

*– Frederick Bravey, Executive Director of a technology company*

"It might feel slightly isolating if you are freelance. You don't always get the work, so there's a lot of time that goes into creating what you consider to be the best you can make, and that the client would definitely want. But if they don't, you may feel rejected. That is all part of being freelance and being self-employed."

*– Patricia Francis, filmmaker*

## Exercise: Would Working for Myself Suit Me?

Referring to the pros and cons set out by Prospects and Reed, plus the quotes above, list three pros and three cons in the table below regarding working for yourself. This should be written from your *own point of view*, for example:

Cons: "I don't like the idea of unpredictable working hours. I would prefer a 9 to 5 job with a healthy work–life balance."

End this activity by saying why working for yourself would suit you, or otherwise.

| Pros | Cons |
|------|------|
|      |      |

**Why working for myself would/would not suit me:**

# Specific Skills and Qualities Required for Working for Yourself

In Chapter 3 we discussed the skills and qualities needed for working in the media and creative industries in general. However, working for yourself will require a certain set of skills, qualities and characteristics. These all relate to risk-taking. Risk-taking can be exciting, and a positive way of trying something new and unexplored. Rook (2019: 267) lists these skills as:

- enterprise and the ability to innovate
- enthusiasm and commitment
- the willingness (and capacity) to work hard
- the ability to deal with pressure and stress
- the flexibility and adaptability to deal with a wide range of issues and problems
- stamina
- self-discipline
- the capacity to learn from new experiences
- the ability to communicate and build networks
- the ability to cope with setbacks and rejection

## Hear from the Experts

"I've recently needed to employ some staff and although education is one thing, there are soft skills that I really do look for in people. These people tend to be quite good leaders. Being confident, and being able to speak in public are important skills. You are most certainly going to need to be organised. That is absolutely crucial. One thing I've found that really helps keep everything on track is to create a routine that you stick to and follow from early morning all the way through to the evening and you go to sleep at the right time. A healthy lifestyle will have a direct impact on your company's growth. You'll find yourself being able to accomplish more tasks during the day when you have a solid routine."

*– Frederick Bravey, Executive Director of a technology company*

"You have to have a real belief in what your work is about. Be resilient, that's really important. You need to find a way of being assertive and showing confidence. In effect, you are selling something. You are trying to get the client to buy something from you. So be confident because they will buy from someone who is confident about the product."

*– Patricia Francis, filmmaker*

# Self-promotion and Self-preservation

In Chapter 8 we will give you advice and guidance on building your own brand, which is essential for freelancers who need to maintain a public profile to promote their services and skills. In addition, Grade (2020: 5) argues that your reputation in the form of recommendations from colleagues and clients is also something you need to maintain, so it is important to prove you have a pleasant personality and are reliable.

Self-employment can put a lot of demands on your life. As mentioned earlier, you are responsible for all areas of your job (from networking to managing finances), and this can pervade all hours of your day. Therefore, you need to know how to relax and avoid burnout.

## Hear from the Experts

"You cannot do everything, and I found that out the hard way. I burnt myself out a few times. There are some things you have to admit that you're not perfect at yet, so you need to identify your flaws and delegate the tasks appropriately. Or you need to hire somebody who's able to take over. By hiring the right people for your company, you will build the right team, and by doing so, you will see exceptional growth."

*– Frederick Bravey, Executive Director of a technology company*

"I don't think I've ever really experienced burnout, but I guess you have just got to get that balance, particularly [if you are] self-employed. You do take your work home with you. You can't help it because you're always thinking. So just make sure you have got that balance. I run so that's my way of having time to myself. And I've got family as well. So obviously that's the way I do it, but I also don't take things too seriously. Life will always go on is my kind of motto. If the camera breaks or something like that, it's not the end of the world. Life will always go on, so there'll be another day."

*– Ben Newth, Head of Video at a corporate video company*

One of the ways you can help yourself when embarking on a self-employed career is to seek out advice and support from a mentor. In the previous chapter you made connections with a mentor during the career case study exercise. You can go through the same process here in finding a mentor who works for themselves.

There are quite a few examples of organisations that support networking and that offer specialised mentoring and other support services that you can access as somebody who works for yourself. The examples below focus specifically on self-employment, but others are listed in Chapter 2.

- Association of Independent Professionals and the Self Employed (IPSE) (ipse.co.uk) – a professional association for the self-employed

- The Design Trust (thedesigntrust.co.uk) – an online business school for designers, makers and professional creative business owners
- Enterprise Nation (enterprisenation.com) – advice and support to start and grow a business
- The Freelancer Club (freelancerclub.net) – a network offering support for freelancers in the creative industries
- Producers Alliance for Cinema and Television (PACT) (pact.co.uk) – an organisation for independent film and television producers
- Production Base (productionbase.co.uk) – a networking organisation for freelancers

# Networking, Pitching and Professional Branding

The art of networking and pitching for work is a particular area of skill that you will need to develop when working for yourself. We will cover pitching, which is something you will do a lot of if you are operating as a freelancer, in Chapter 9. As we discussed above when we talked about the skills and qualities required for the self-employed, reputation management is key. Being able to present your brand in a professional way is very important. Managing your **digital footprint** and **professional branding** will be covered in Chapter 8.

## Hear from the Expert

"A lot of it is word of mouth. A lot of freelancers worked for production companies prior to going freelance so you knew of them and you knew of their work. But at the same time we also kind of get cold calls or emails from freelancers introducing themselves and if there's a link in there to their work and their work looks good, then we will always put them on file or contact them just to let them know that we like what we saw and then we kind of talk a bit more. Just see if there's some sort of connection there and then we start to talk about day rates and things like that. It might be six months down the line before we actually use that person. But yeah, we have basically got a database, but the onus is very much on the freelancer to put themselves out there really and let the world know that they exist. Start publishing your content and stuff like that, and just start making a noise. Basically, tell the world that you're there."

*– Ben Newth, Head of Video at a corporate video company*

# Self-employment: Starting Now!

It is not uncommon for students to be working for themselves during their studies. This is something you can consider if you have ambitions to be self-employed in your future career.

Here are a few things you can work on in preparation for self-employment:

- identify and list some of the things you are already doing that you can develop further into a more formal area of paid work (for example, DJing, photography, videography, social media marketing)
- gather together examples of your work that you can use to promote yourself (videos, photos, podcasts, marketing campaigns, reports), which can be from work experience or from your course content
- work on your **professional branding** (website, portfolio, social media, photobook, showreel) to promote your work
- connect with your university's centre for enterprise for support, guidance and potential funding
- network with fellow students who are also working for themselves while at university

---

### Student Voice

"I do uni work in the week and then for weekends I just do content creation. It sort of feels like living two lives a little bit, but they blend together on so many other levels and it just works for me. As long as you manage your time and look out for yourself. You can't really go wrong."

*– Shakirah Jelley, Digital Content Creator*

---

## Exercise: Matching Skills and Qualities Developed at University With Skills Needed for Working for Yourself

We have given a brief insight above into some of the skills and qualities you will need when working for yourself. You are already exercising many of these skills and qualities on your degree course. Let's think for a moment which skills you are developing while at university that might indicate that you have the qualities to help you succeed when working for yourself.

Use the table below to identify five skills and qualities needed for working for yourself. In the left-hand column, name the skill and/or quality needed; in the right-hand column give some evidence of how you have demonstrated this during your course. You should refer to some of the examples highlighted by Rook (2019) in the list above to help you.

For example:

| Skills and qualities needed | Evidence from your course |
| --- | --- |
| The capacity to learn from new experiences | On an occasion when I was working with a group of peers whom I had not met before, I showed capacity to learn from this experience. I did this through demonstrating what I could offer the team and appreciating what others could contribute too. |

| Skills and qualities needed | Evidence from your course |
| --- | --- |

Follow this up by answering the following questions:

- Which skills and qualities are you developing that you already feel confident about?
- Which ones might need further development?
- How will you achieve this?

# Researching Working for Yourself

If you decide that working for yourself might suit you when you graduate, or even while you are still a student, you are advised to research the list below. Grade's (2020) *Freelance Toolkit* is a valuable resource to help with this. You could also contact your university's centre for enterprise for help with this research.

- financial skills – you are responsible for keeping records of income and expenditure
- understanding the UK tax system – you are responsible for registering yourself with HMRC and completing your tax return each year
- appreciating the value of your labour – a pay rate is determined on skills and experience and knowing how to negotiate with a client
- holiday pay – research your entitlement to paid holiday leave. For example, workers who are in employment for a full leave year are entitled to a specified amount of statutory leave. Those who are employed on short-term contracts should be paid for untaken holiday in lieu

- invoicing – an invoice is a legally binding document that you use to bill your client. You should research how to put one together and how to present it to your client
- pensions – research your position with regard to pensions and seek the help of a qualified financial adviser. Don't assume that you can leave this until you are older

## Hear from the Experts

"Making sure that commercially you're making money, or at least breaking even, is important. If working for yourself, make sure you understand your accounts and the financial side of things. If you don't have a grasp on it, make sure you find someone you can rely on that can do that for you."

*– Simon Elliott, Managing Director, Diversity Agency*

"I suppose when you first go into the industry, you're there for creative reasons. Primarily, you want to do something creative. I think when you set up your own business, whether that's a production company or just as a sole trader freelancing, there's a lot more to it than just being creative. And I actually found that I enjoyed the marketing side of it as equally as I did the production side of it. You're a business and you've got to promote yourself. You've got to network and get to know who the movers and shakers in your local area are. And get yourself a good accountant because HMRC won't take ignorance as an excuse. Just get all those pillars in place so that you can focus on why you set the business up in the first place, which was to make videos to make productions."

*– Ben Newth, Head of Video at a corporate video company*

"Without the more 'boring admin stuff' you cannot do all the exciting things. Anybody thinking about working for themselves be aware of the challenging bits of working alone as well. Whether it's your business or someone else's, even if you think you're working on your own, you won't be. I can guarantee if you really think about what you do to get your job done, you'll need at least a customer somewhere, so that's at least one stakeholder and no doubt there will be many more who are needed to make it happen. Having these people and admin skills is relevant whichever direction you go in."

*– Simon Elliott, Managing Director, Diversity Agency*

## Conclusion

In this chapter we have explored the idea of working for yourself. As we mentioned at the beginning of the chapter, the nature of the media and creative industries and its project-based employment means that you are likely to encounter some freelancing work at some point in your career. We have highlighted some of the personal skills and qualities you will need to foster, such as resilience, drive and the ability to create networks. We have also asked you to think about some of the pros and cons so that you have a realistic outlook on this type of work.

In the next few chapters of the book, we look at placements and help you to start making plans for work experience while on your course. In Chapter 6 we define work experience and help to find the right placement for you.

## Further Reading

Davies, Rosamund, and Sigthorsson, Gauti (2013) *Introducing the Creative Industries: From Theory to Practice*. London: Sage. Refer to this book for further information on freelancing and self-employment in the creative industries.

Gov.uk (n.d.) 'Business and self-employed: Tools and guidance for business'. *Gov.uk* [website]. www.gov.uk/browse/business. Refer to the UK Government website for general advice on self-employment and freelancing.

Grade, Alison (2020) 'The Freelance Toolkit' (3rd edition).Available at: https://www. screenskills.com/media/4092/freelance-tooolkit-10122020.pdf. This is a guide for people setting out on careers in film, TV, visual effects, animation and games.

Rook, Steve (2019) *The Graduate Career Guidebook: Advice for Students and Graduates on Career Options, Jobs, Volunteering, Applications, Interviews, and Self-Employment*. Basingstoke: Palgrave Macmillan. This book has a useful section on self-employment.

Smith, Jemma (2023, May) 'Create a great video CV'. *Prospects* [website]. www.prospects. ac.uk/careers-advice/cvs-and-cover-letters/create-a-great-video-cv

# 6

# DEFINING WORK EXPERIENCE

## Finding the Right Placement for You

## Introduction

In the previous few chapters of this book, we introduced you to finding out what type of work is available in the media and creative industries. We enabled you to analyse the world of work, research potential career areas, and also helped you to consider freelancing and working for yourself. Now you have this insight into what the media and creative industries are, it is time to start thinking about gaining some real experience in the form of finding a placement. This chapter will help to enlighten you on where to look for **work experience** and also to reveal types of work experience that you may not have considered before.

The aims and outcomes of this chapter are:

* to consider what work experience is
* to consider the benefits of having work experience
* to explore where you might look for work experience

List of exercises in this chapter:

* Undertaking an audit of previous work experience
* Considering the value of work experience
* Using SMART objectives for your work experience
* Conducting an interview with a previous placement student on your course

# What is Work Experience?

Work experience may sometimes be described as an **internship** or a **placement** but, at its simplest level, it can be thought of as 'experience of work'. It is any paid or unpaid work undertaken, including voluntary work. BECTU's (Broadcasting, Entertainment, Communications and Theatre Union) (n.d.) *Creative Toolkit* says that:

> Students or others on work experience should be given the chance to try various tasks and develop skills … but they should not be relied upon to fulfil roles that are necessary for the organisation and would otherwise be undertaken by members of staff.

A wide range of activities can count as work experience, and you have probably already had quite a lot of experience of work which it is worth reflecting on here. The following exercise will help you to understand what might be defined as work experience.

## Exercise: Undertaking an Audit of Previous Work Experience

Complete the following exercise in order to 'audit' what you have already done in terms of work experience. Read through the list below, identifying the different types of work experience you have engaged with already.

Types of work experience:

- paid part-time work while in education, such as work in hospitality
- placement/s undertaken during school
- working during the summer holidays
- volunteering for a local charity
- self-employment, such as photographic assignments for live events
- clubs and societies you belong to, such as being part of a sports team
- political or campaign group activity you might be involved with
- work shadowing, such as visiting an organisation for a day
- simulations and live projects in education, such as producing a video for a local organisation
- social media activity, such as blog writing, vlogging, podcasting, hosting a video channel

Hopefully, this audit will highlight the fact that you already have quite a lot of work experience. It may also help you to begin to focus on your interest areas, on the skills you already have and on the ones you might want to develop further. There may be examples of work experience you would rather not repeat in future and organisations you would like to revisit for a more in-depth placement. Consider how this might inform your search for work experience during your course.

# The Value of Work Experience

We now recommend that you build on the exercise above by continuing to find work experience relevant to your course and your future ambitions. During your degree course it is recommended that you engage with a variety of different work experiences. This can help you to discover what you would like to do in your future career and, perhaps, what you want to avoid. Rook (2016) highlights the following five points that work experience offers you:

- researching a role – getting a deeper understanding of sectors and how they link to your goals and aspirations
- developing your skills – building a portfolio of relevant experience
- building contacts – creating a network of potential employers and colleagues
- undertaking experience required – having the relevant amount of experience in the role to apply for graduate jobs
- opening doors – getting your foot in the door

(adapted from Rook, 2016: 14–15)

The next exercise will help you to consider the value of work experience to you personally.

## Exercise: Considering the Value of Work Experience

Look at the table below listing the benefits of engaging with work experience during your degree course. Pick out what you consider to be the top five reasons to engage with work experience. Arrange them in order from 1 to 5 with the most important being at the top of the list. You can reflect on these benefits for the next exercise where you will be setting personal objectives for work experience.

| | | |
|---|---|---|
| To gain an understanding of the world of work | To gain relevant experience in a specific field of employment that I might be interested in | To create contacts and networks in the field |
| To gain an insight into different workplace cultures | To practise and enhance my communication and presentation skills | To find potential jobs and career areas |
| To develop and practise using a range of skills relevant to the world of work | To reinforce skills that I already have | To enhance my CV so I will be able to cite relevant work experience on it |
| To earn some money if it is a paid placement | To apply my degree course to a practical workplace context | To contribute towards my final-year dissertation project as a case study |

*(Continued)*

| | | |
|---|---|---|
| To test my time management and organisational skills | To practise at job hunting, using my CV, writing a cover letter/email, making applications and having interviews | To get a foot in the door and possibly lead to a full-time graduate job |
| To check whether my chosen sector suits me | To work in a team in a workplace context | To boost my confidence |
| To develop my personal qualities, such as independence and self-presentation | To experience life beyond the 'university bubble' | To put myself ahead of my graduating cohort in terms of the labour market |

| Order of importance to you | Top five reasons to engage in work experience |
|---|---|
| 1 = most important | |
| 2 | |
| 3 | |
| 4 | |
| 5 | |

## Hear from the Experts

"Experience is so important. The job with DeCantillon was a lot of fun, but it's not exactly what I want to do. That's another thing: don't hold out for only applying for jobs that you know you really want. If it's going to get your foot in the door, if it's going to get you in the industry, do it. It means you are in and your name is in so it's more likely people will contact you for certain jobs, and you can grow from there. Most of us know that a runner job is one of the most common ways of entering the industry but there are lots of other opportunities out there for people breaking into the industry so don't limit yourself."
– *Laura Savage, Marketing Director, DeCantillon Films*

"Whenever I talk to students about maximising placement success, I use my career as a bit of a case study because if it wasn't for my placements, I wouldn't be where I am right now. I'm a big advocate of placements and internships. I think it's often underestimated just how far they can take you in the future, whether that's through the people you meet, or through the skills that you learn. Placements unlock the door to real-world experience that you can't access anywhere else in the early stages of your career."
– *Tom Walters, Account Director, The Dairy*

"After I graduated, I decided that I didn't want to go straight into the industry. People want experience and it's tough when you graduate, you think 'yes, I've got this degree, great', and then you see job listings after job listings that say 'we want a degree and experience'. This is incredibly frustrating when you know that you likely don't have the experience that employers are looking for. Experience is really important. If you can get as much experience as possible now, while you're getting your degree, then that will really improve your chances. Try and get something as soon as you can. You can pursue other things at the same time as well. I recently launched a site where I create recipes for baked goods based on films and TV shows called 'Flavour of the Film' (@ flavourofthefilm). I work on my recipes alongside any other work I'm doing within the industry, and I find it really fulfilling."

*– Laura Savage, Marketing Director, DeCantillon Films*

# Setting Objectives for Your Work Experience

Having established the value of work experience we will now encourage you to develop some objectives which define what you would like to gain from any work experience that you are engaged in. It might be, for example, that you want to stretch yourself by trying out tasks you haven't done before (working with clients, talking to customers over the phone, helping with the organisation of a live event, etc.), or by developing your **soft skills**, such as working under your own initiative, problem-solving, meeting deadlines and communicating with others. Thinking about how to meet these goals may influence the type of placement you look for. The exercise below will help you with this.

## Exercise: Using Smart Objectives for Your Work Experience

For this exercise we recommend that you develop a record of your objectives for future work experience. These can be based on the value of work experience you identified in the previous exercise.

Each of these objectives for work experience should be written up in a short paragraph following the **SMART objectives** set out as follows:

S – Specific (name a specific activity or skill that you are aiming for)

M – Measurable (How will you know/demonstrate that you have achieved this aim? Will it be measurable through placement provider feedback, for instance?)

A – Achievable (select something that you know is achievable within the constraints of the work experience)

R – Realistic/Relevant (discuss how your objectives are relevant to building a particular skillset or career aspiration)

T – Timely or Time-bound (decide on a date or deadline by which you can say you have reached this goal)

For example:

> "I am aiming to boost my confidence. This will be measured by speaking
> out more, offering help, or giving my opinion. I know that this is something
> I can realistically achieve and demonstrate if I can do so by the end of my
> placement."

It is worth spending some time on writing these SMART objectives as it will be useful for career development in future. You will be able to use them to inform the writing of your CV and cover letter/email, and your job applications, so it is a very useful writing skill to have. They will also inform the content of your **placement report**, which we discuss in Chapter 12, and in developing your career plan, which is the topic of Chapter 13.

We recommend that you refer to these objectives when searching for placements. Update and refine your objectives over time and whenever relevant.

---

## Hear from the Experts

"I think for students it's almost an essential, a necessity really, that they should try and get some sort of experience. It can make or break your career. I could've ended up in a career that I didn't enjoy, had it not been for my placements."

*– Tom Walters, Account Director, The Dairy*

"A placement not only shows you what you do like, but also what you don't like, so it's really useful."

*– Noushka Seher, International Account Manager*

---

# Finding Work Experience and Self-sourcing a Placement

We have considered the benefits of doing work experience in general and have recommended that you engage with a variety of experiences during your degree, either as part of your degree course or as extra-curricular activity. It may be a series of short-term placements or something more long term, such as a sandwich year. We are now going to help you to work your way through the process of finding a placement and planning for it.

Your university will have a careers department to assist you in finding your placement, or it may be the case that a tutor will make work experience available as part of an assignment. It is clear, however, that the more independence you are given in securing work experience, the better for you in the long run. For example, even if you are being supported by your university, you may still have to research, source and apply for a placement. You may have to pitch for it or give a presentation as part of a shortlist of candidates to secure the placement. All of this will give you real experience that will help prepare you for graduation and the first steps into your career journey. You may also decide to completely self-source your placement. We will now consider the main sources you can access to scout for work experience.

## Look at Your Own Network

One way to self-source a placement is to look at your own network. Consider as many contacts as you can think of in the categories below and think about whether any of these people might have an appropriate opportunity for you:

*   family and relations
*   friends and friends of friends
*   social groups you belong to
*   work colleagues from an existing part-time job
*   peers/fellow students' contacts
*   alumni from your course
*   tutors on your course
*   social media connections

## Changing the Focus of an Existing Job

You can also self-source a placement by changing the focus of a pre-existing job. For example, if you work on the checkout of a supermarket, you can consider asking about working with the company's Public Relations and Marketing department/Head Office/ Advertising Agency. You are already on the books as an employee so many of the health and safety and Human Resources (HR) requirements are covered and this type of work may lead to further opportunities in future.

## Make a Speculative Application

You can source a placement through making a speculative application. Not all place-ments are advertised, so sometimes it is a matter of making enquiries and seeing if work experience is available. Look for organisations you'd like to work with and see if they have any opportunities. If you cannot find any work experience or placements being advertised, you can contact an employer from the organisation to express your interest.

## Volunteering

Work experience does not always have to be formal work that would otherwise pay a sal-ary. Consider volunteering as an opportunity to gain some relevant experience of work. Your university will have systems in place to encourage community engagement. It may also take part in the annual Volunteering Week scheme. Some of the types of volunteering that are available can include:

- languages – helping international students develop language skills and feel at home
- food – working for a local foodbank or as a kitchen volunteer
- the environment – helping out on a community allotment
- sports – organising a sporting event or coaching a team
- hospitals – helping with administration, fundraising or community engagement

(Adapted from targetjobs.co.uk)

Doit.life (https://doit.life/volunteer) is a website that enables volunteering. It lists volunteering opportunities nationwide, so there may be something you can find to do in your hometown as well as your place of study.

## Your Student Union

You could consider working with the Student Union at your university. If you already belong to a club or society, maybe you can get some experience offering to work as their Social Media Manager or Events Coordinator, for example. Your university may have a selection of media societies, such as a student magazine, radio station or TV channel. Other opportunities can include working as an academic rep for your course, working as an equality and diversity officer, or as a National Union of Students (NUS) delegate. These types of opportunities are usually filled early on in the academic calendar, so look out for them at the start of your course, or at the beginning of the first term each year.

## Self-employment

If you are interested in self-employment, you can explore the possibility of making this the focus of your work experience placement. It could be based on an enterprise you are currently involved in, and your placement could focus on building that business further. If you are not currently involved in something like this but are interested in self-employment, you can seek support and help from your university's enterprise department. (See Chapter 5 for more information on self-employment.)

## Placement Search Websites

You can consult the following websites, which offer more general types of work experience, to look for placements:

- milkround.com
- targetjobs.co.uk
- E4s.co.uk

- jobs.theguardian.com
- ratemyplacement.co.uk
- uk.indeed.com
- REED.co.uk

The list below names websites that are specifically focused on the media and creative industries:

- careers.channel4.com/4skills/work-experience – this section of the Channel 4 website offers work experience opportunities
- @BBCGetIn (Instagram and Twitter/X) – provides updates and insights into opportunities for new talent, including work experience opportunities at the BBC
- careers.sky.com – the 'early careers' section of the Sky website has information on internships and placements
- creativeaccess.org.uk – this is a website that supports underrepresented communities in the creative industries and lists internship opportunities
- freelancevideocollective.com – this is a network for production companies and freelance filmmakers for film and TV jobs. You can sign up to search for available internships
- itvjobs.com – there is a section for work experience at ITV on the website. You can also follow social media channels @itvlovestalent for opportunities
- mediabeans.io – a website that includes opportunities for internships and training and work experience
- shootingpeople.org – a community of filmmakers who collaborate to produce independent films which may provide possible placement opportunities
- tvcrewfinder.com – a website for freelancers and producers to crew for TV work, which may be a place to search for work experience opportunities
- tvwatercooler.org – a list of media companies offering work experience nationwide. You can search for the page on companies offering work experience schemes

Remember also to look at some of the sites that focus specifically on advice for careers in the media and creative industries, including:

- screenskills.com – a membership organisation for careers support and training around work experience in the screen industries
- bectu.org.uk – a membership organisation/union that offers training and networking opportunities and offers useful advice about freelancing and work experience
- discovercreative.careers – this website has a section listing opportunities, including placements, workshops, courses and paid internships
- guru.bafta.org – a hub for career advice which includes an opportunities section that lists masterclasses, competitions, showcases and scholarships

Of particular use here is LinkedIn. You can use it for searching for work experience opportunities among the network you are developing. You are advised to set your profile as being 'available for work' for the duration of your search. You should also identify in your headline section the sort of work experience you are interested in. We will be offering more detailed advice on setting up a LinkedIn profile in Chapter 8.

---

( **Hear from the Expert** )───────────────────────────

"In terms of looking for work experience opportunities, my main advice would be to look at a website called Media Beans, the BBC/ITV/Global/Bauer websites and social media feeds, as well as the Student Radio Association's Facebook groups and Twitter/X pages. You've got to keep a look out for opportunities as they won't just come to you."

*– Emma Snow, Journalist, BBC*

---

## Cultural Quarters

Many cities have networks and support groups set up in their Cultural Quarter (sometimes referred to as a Creative or Digital Quarter or Media City). These tend to be a hub for creative businesses where appropriate work experience may be found. Again, this could be something to investigate in your place of study or nearer to your hometown.

## Careers Fairs and Employer Presentations

Your university's careers team will organise careers fairs and employer presentations. Check your university's careers website for updates during your placement search. Make sure you regularly check emails for bulletins of careers fairs and other events, such as invitations to see guest speakers. These are the types of events where employers will outline their career area and give information on how to get a foot in the door. Some will offer placements too. You could also consider approaching a guest speaker at the end of an event to express your interest in gaining some work experience.

There are also a number of national virtual employability events and careers fairs where you can look for placement opportunities. These include the list below, but you are advised to research others that are relevant to your career area of interest:

* ratemyplacement.co.uk – virtual events and webinars
* rts.org.uk – Royal Television Society careers fairs
* screenskills.com – virtual events and webinars

## Remote Placements

Many industries have employers who work remotely or in a hybrid form of working that combines office work and working from home (especially so since the Covid-19 pandemic). Many organisations have converted previous face-to-face placements into remote ones, or they have found a new way of working which means some placements are more suitable to being carried out from home.

It is possible to get a lot out of a remote placement. For example, you may be given specific, focused tasks to perform rather than to shadow somebody. The nature of the media and creative industries also means that roles in **digital marketing** or producing content for social media can be easily carried out remotely, as long as you have the technology to do so and can have regular online meetings with the placement provider to give you support and feedback.

# Other Opportunities for Developing Your Work Experience

You could consider gaining valuable work experience through exploring a broader definition of what counts as work experience. The list below of **work-related learning** (WRL) will give you some ideas about how you can do this.

- Live projects – you could negotiate a brief for a project with an employer as your work experience placement (for example, producing a video or social media content for an organisation)
- Community-engaged learning and outreach projects – you could negotiate with a local community organisation for a problem-based project to complete within an agreed time frame
- Competitions, festivals and events – you could enter your work (a film or video of yours, for example) into a competition, festival or showcase. The work you do in preparing the film and entering it would be a rich opportunity for skills development
- Hackathons – a hackathon is a web-based challenge focused on a set theme. There are lots of types of hackathons that focus on different industries and sectors, and with some detailed research online you may be able to sign up to one that suits you. This could make for a suitable work experience opportunity, particularly if you are interested in coding, design and app development
- Incubators and start-ups – these are remote working projects set up by small start-up companies that do not have space in their work premises for a placement student. You could search your local cultural or creative quarter for potential organisations to work with
- Study for a course – studying for a course that specifically builds your skills in a particular area could count for work experience. You can find appropriate courses online (for example, on LinkedIn Learning, ScreenSkills, Google's Digital Garage) and most will offer you a certificate which confirms the number of hours you spent on the course. You could add such certificates to your social media profiles, CV and portfolio.

─( **Hear from the Expert** )──────────────────────

"Don't wait until graduation. Do what you can do now rather than waiting till graduation. As an employer, whether it be freelancer or full time, you look for people that haven't sat on their *****. They've gone out and been proactive. They've thought about what they could do, whether that's creating content themselves, volunteering somewhere, just anything like that that you can put on a CV or put in an email that shows us that you haven't just sat around waiting to graduate. You've actually got a bit of experience. You know what a camera looks like. You know what software people are using, just anything that kind of makes you stand out from the crowd. The more proactive you can be [is] definitely the better, because it would just make you stand out from the crowd a bit more."

*– Ben Newth, Head of Video at a corporate video company*

── **Student Voice** ──────────────────────

"Try not to get overwhelmed and use your resources. It's not worth getting stressed out over, finding a placement is supposed to be fun and exciting. If you are struggling with your search, talk to your university's support services, or ask your tutors to put you in touch with students who have previously completed placements, that are willing to mentor you through the process. Asking for help will get you a lot further than trying to figure it out on your own!"

*– Emily May Drummond, Media Production student*

# Previous Work Experience On Your Degree Course

As you can see from the vast array of opportunities and avenues outlined in this chapter, there are many possibilities for you to source some work experience during your time at university. Before embarking on your search, you might benefit from finding out what types of work experience previous students have done on your degree. The following exercise will enable you to conduct some research into this. It may give you some leads into where you can find your own work experience or placement.

## Exercise: Conducting an Interview with a Previous Student on Your Course

Locate a student from the year group above you and interview them about a placement they have been engaged with (your tutor may be able to help you with this). You can use the sorts of questions listed below:

- What did you do for your placement?
- What was the name of the employer?

- How and where did you find the work experience?
- What was your job role?
- What was the job description?
- What were your main objectives for doing the work experience?
- What did you learn from the experience?
- Is there anything you would do differently if you were to do it again?
- How do you plan to use this experience in the future?
- Do you have any specific tips, hints and advice about work experience?

Think about how you will use this information to inform your own search for work experience. What are the main points you have learned from talking to this student and hearing their advice'?

# Conclusion

Hopefully, by the end of this chapter you have gained an insight into the variety of different forms that work experience can take. We have defined what is meant by 'work experience' and given examples of how it can include anything from community volunteering to contributing to a university society or working remotely from home.

We have given you ideas of where you might look for a placement. You have also set yourselves some SMART objectives in readiness for your work experience.

In the next chapter we are going to start preparing you for your work experience by helping you to refine your CV and cover letter/email in readiness for making applications.

## Further Reading

Fanthome, Christine (2005) *Work Placements: A Survival Guide for Students*. London: Springer Nature. This book is a step-by-step guide to help students apply, interview and get the most out of placements. It provides insights into employers' and tutors' perspectives, and lists employability skills that are sought by employers.

Helyer, R., and Lee, D. (2014) 'The role of work experience in the future employability of Higher Education graduates'. *Higher Education Quarterly*, 68(3), 348–372. This academic article provides an insight into the role of experiential learning through work experience.

Rook, Steve (2016) *Work Experience, Placements and Internships*. Palgrave Study Skills Series. Basingstoke: Palgrave Macmillan. This is a good all-rounder which goes into detail about some of the suggestions raised in this chapter. Chapter 1 of Rook's book explains 'why experience matters'.

# 7

# DEVELOPING MATERIALS FOR WORK EXPERIENCE

## Preparing Your CV, Cover Letter/ Email and Making Applications

## Introduction

In the previous chapter, we introduced you to the wide range of work experience opportunities available to you during your degree course. This chapter will now focus on developing your career materials, namely your CV and cover letter/email, in order to apply for work experience. It will also be useful practice for the future. We are assuming that you have already written a basic CV. It could be one that you have produced for previous work experience or work. The purpose of this chapter is to enhance and tailor it.

The chapter aims to help you:

- develop a CV that is appropriate for making applications for work experience in the media and creative industries
- discover how to target your CV and cover letter/email to make a successful application
- produce a CV and cover letter/email for use in applying for your work experience

List of exercises in this chapter:

- Building your CV
- Peer reviewing your CV
- Producing your cover letter/email

Your CV is one of the most important tools you have in your possession in your search for work experience, and later on in your search for work. Besides the initial email or call you make to your placement provider/employer, the CV will be one of the first points of communication you have to introduce and create an impression of yourself. It is important that your CV has impact, is concise yet detailed, and that it is appropriate and tailored for the job you are applying for. The information and exercises in this chapter will enable you to make your CV bespoke to your applications for work experience.

## Hear from the Expert

"Keeping an up-to-date CV is really important, especially if you're actively looking for work or unhappy in the role that you're in at the moment. It means that you have a template ready for when a new opportunity arrives and you can capitalise on it. A lot of job recruitment opportunities have tight deadlines so having a CV ready means that you can focus more on your cover letter and interview preparation, which strengthens your application as a whole."

*– Jacob Germany, Videographer*

## Student Voices

"For me, keeping an up-to-date CV is essential in career development. My advice would be to keep your CV and personal development at the forefront of your mind when completing tasks and working on projects. Reflect on the skills and attributes you have developed and add them into your CV! In my current role, I find myself working on a variety of projects, all enabling me to develop various skills within different areas of marketing. I aim to revisit my CV on a monthly basis to update any areas which I think I have progressed from the previous month."

*– Michael Goulding, Graduate Development Programme student*

"Keeping an up-to-date CV is a great way to ensure you are always prepared either to send or update your best CV to potential employers and, if you are like me, reduces the overall stress of applying for a job! It is as easy as adding any recent employment history, training, or achievements either to an existing CV or on a separate document. You can then pick and choose what experiences will best suit certain applications. This will ensure that you are not missing any game-changing information that certain employers could be looking for (e.g. completing training for a specific industry-level camera). Plus, updating your CV can be a confidence booster, legitimatising your achievements and talents for your own sense of self."

*– Callum Roome, postgraduate media student*

# Targeting Your CV

You need to start by targeting your CV towards particular jobs or career areas. One way of doing this is by emphasising or drawing attention to the most appropriate aspects of your experience that are relevant to the chosen job. For example, if you are the president of a society at university, you can foreground that to highlight your leadership skills. If you have taken part in an assignment that involved working to an external client brief, make sure it is prominent on the page because it can be categorised as work experience.

If, however, your experience of employment is limited to hospitality, translate the tasks you carry out at work into skills, such as:

- teamwork
- customer-facing
- working under your own initiative
- time-keeping

Some of these skills will no doubt be mentioned as 'essential' or 'desirable' in the job adverts you have found.

Once you have gained experience in targeting your CV in this way, you should find it simple to adapt and redraft your CV for specific jobs as you apply for work experience. You can even keep several versions of your CV to hand if this makes the process of targeting it simpler.

There are numerous online apps and templates to help you create and organise your CV. You can use one of these to make a start with your CV and then move on to refine it further by following the tips below. It is also worth checking with your university careers department as they are there to offer help and support too. The careers department might offer CV workshops or one-to-one drop-in appointments that you can use to your advantage.

There are many different types of CV, including chronological ones that follow your career in date order, but the most appropriate type for an undergraduate with limited work experience is a skills-based or competency-based CV. This is a good technique for students who want to highlight the skills and qualities and other experience they have acquired.

## Exercise: Building Your CV

In this exercise you will build and target your CV based on the guidelines and tips we offer below. You should start by finding a job you are interested in applying for. In Chapter 4 you performed a mock job hunt. You can use the live job advert that you found for that exercise as the basis for creating or enhancing your CV. Once you have completed this exercise, compare and contrast your previous CV alongside the newly targeted one to see how it has developed.

# Guidelines on Writing Your CV

In this section we give you some guidelines on writing a successful CV for applications for jobs in the media and creative industries.

Start by creating a file and naming and dating it so that it is easily identifiable. This makes it easy for you and employers to identify the file. Start the document itself with your full name at the top of the page. Add your town or city rather than your full address for reasons of privacy and provide your professional email address and/or your contact number.

For reasons of equal opportunities, privacy and to avoid identity theft, you do not need to include details such as your age and date of birth, your gender or marital status. For the same reason, you would not usually include a photo of yourself either. In this section, ensure that you include links to your professional social media, such as LinkedIn, Instagram and media sharing sites. (We will be focusing more on professional social media and branding in Chapter 8.)

## Personal Statement

Next, write a personal statement. This should be a short paragraph of two or three lines about who you are and your current skills. It should also provide an indication of the sort of work you are interested in. For example, a videographer looking for work in the field of sports journalism; a social media marketing assistant looking for work in the field of fashion marketing; a video editor interested in working in the music industry. Your personal statement should be based on the details of the job you are applying for.

## Key Skills

The next section is about **key skills**. This is a bulleted list which picks out some of the skills listed in the job advert that you are targeting your CV to. The list might include specific equipment and software skills and a range of **generic skills** and personal qualities. You should provide some evidence to demonstrate that you possess the skill and an example for each key skill you have listed (for example, a producer on a university group video project). Where possible, it is useful to be able to indicate how much experience you have. For example, how many projects you have worked on as a producer. Refer to Chapter 3 regarding skills, qualities, attributes and behaviours for further inspiration on this part of your CV.

## Work Experience

The work experience section of your CV gives you the opportunity to make a bulleted list of any relevant work experience you already have. You should list this in reverse chronological order with the most recent first. For each item of work experience you list, you should briefly explain your job description and set out the transferable skills relevant to the position you are aiming your CV at. Remember that a project brief from a real client and any volunteering you have done counts as work experience too.

## Hobbies and Interests

You may want to have a section about your hobbies and interests, but it is best to only include these where they are directly relevant to the job you are applying for. If you do mention them, always provide examples and evidence of their relevance to the position you are applying for.

## Education and Training

Next, list your education, in reverse chronological order, putting your current course first. Identify some modules that are relevant to your application too. When listing previous education, keep it brief, stating the number of qualifications and highlighting only the important ones. Always include your A levels or BTECs. For example, 10 GCSEs including Media, English and Maths. Remember to mention the names of the institutions and the dates you attended. This should be presented as a bulleted list.

Relevant training comes next. This can include a bulleted list of any training you have undertaken that is relevant to the post. For example, technical training, first aid and health and safety training, a driving licence and any LinkedIn Learning or ScreenSkills certificates you have gained. For each bit of training, you should give the exact name of the course and the date you completed it.

## References

The CV should give details of at least one **referee** who can vouch for your skills and suitability for the position you are applying for by providing a **reference**. This could be a university tutor or a former or current employer. You will need to provide the referee's name, job role and the organisation they work for, along with their email address. Make sure you ask them for permission to include their details beforehand. If you are not writing your referee's contact details on the CV itself, you can state 'references available on request'. We will be giving more advice on how you obtain references after having gained more work experience in Chapter 13.

## GDPR Statement

Finally, a **GDPR (General Data Protection Regulation) statement** should be added as a footer of the CV document. It should read 'This CV may be kept on file and distributed for employment purposes' and gives permission for your CV to be distributed to other potential employers.

# Tips and Hints on CV Writing

It is important to recognise that there is no definitive way of producing or designing a CV. Each CV is unique and dependent on its specific context. The tips and hints below are some general pieces of advice. You should seek further specific and personalised advice from your university's careers advisors. In order to get a sense of what is most appropriate, you can search online for examples of CVs in similar career areas to your own.

- Your CV should usually be no more than two pages long and saved as a PDF document to protect its formatting
- You should aim to have a smart and clearly presented CV, which uses simple fonts and an uncluttered design. You can use subheadings to separate the different sections of the CV
- Use positive and assertive language throughout the CV with words such as 'managed', 'led', 'accomplished' and 'succeeded'. You should try to reflect the language and tone used in the job advert to which you are targeting your CV
- It is very important that you check for typos and spelling mistakes. Asking a friend to proof-read your CV is always a good idea

## Student Voice

"Employers are always interested in finding out more about the individuals they are looking to hire. An essential section worth including is an 'Additional Skills and Achievements' section. Having this section allows candidates to stand out from the various other applicants as they are able to demonstrate any other activities or achievements they have been involved in, such as charitable work, awards received and hobbies."

*– Michael Goulding, Graduate Development Programme student*

## Exercise: Peer Reviewing Your CV

Once you have written your CV, asking one of your peers to review your CV is an ideal next step. It is always helpful for a fresh pair of eyes to review your CV. Choose someone on your course and swap the CVs you have both produced. If this is not possible, find a trusted friend to review your CV. Even better, consider approaching a potential employer/mentor, perhaps the person you interviewed as part of the case study in Chapter 4, to review your CV. You could give them the CV review form below to complete. Then make any necessary changes based on the feedback you receive.

| Criteria for evaluation of CV | Yes | No | Comments and suggestions on improvements |
|---|---|---|---|
| **Presentation of the CV** | | | |
| Is the CV smartly presented and clearly laid out? | **Yes** | No | |
| Does it make use of subheadings to break up the content? | **Yes** | No | |
| Does it make effective use of short paragraphs and bullet points? | **Yes** | No | |
| Is the typography consistent and appropriate in style? | **Yes** | No | |
| Are there any typos or spelling mistakes? | **Yes** | No | |
| Is there consistent use of positive and assertive language? | **Yes** | No | |

| | **Personal Information** | |
|---|---|---|
| Is the full name of the person included on the CV? | **Yes** | No |
| Does it include the contact details (email/phone number) of the applicant? | **Yes** | No |
| Is the contact email address suitably professional? | **Yes** | No |
| Does the CV include links to professional social media accounts? | **Yes** | No |
| Does it exclude mention of age, gender, marital status, or a photo? | **Yes** | No |
| | **Personal Statement** | |
| Is the profile concise? | **Yes** | No |
| Does the personal statement list the main achievements and skills of the applicant? | **Yes** | No |
| | **Key Skills** | |
| Does the CV list the applicant's key skills? | **Yes** | No |
| Is it clear how the skills listed are appropriate to the job being applied for? | **Yes** | No |
| Are evidence and examples of the key skills provided? | **Yes** | No |
| | **Work Experience** | |
| Does the CV list any work experience relevant to the job being applied for? | **Yes** | No |
| Is the list of work experience in date order with the most recent first? | **Yes** | No |
| Does the list of work experience include details of the employer, including a link to their website? | **Yes** | No |
| Does the list of work experience detail the role and responsibilities, skills developed and key achievements? | **Yes** | No |
| If hobbies and interests are included, is their relevance to the job made clear? | **Yes** | No |
| | **Education and Qualifications** | |
| Is the list of education and qualifications presented in reverse chronological order? | **Yes** | No |
| Does the list of education include the dates attended and names of the institution? | **Yes** | No |
| Does the CV avoid long lists of qualifications and grades? | **Yes** | No |
| Is there mention of the modules studied on the degree course where they are relevant to the job being applied for? | **Yes** | No |
| Is there any mention and evidence of relevant training undertaken? | **Yes** | No |
| | **References** | |
| Does the CV include details of at least one referee, giving their name, employer, job role and contact details? | **Yes** | No |
| If the CV does not include referee details, does it state 'References available upon request'? | **Yes** | No |
| | **GDPR Statement** | |
| Is there a GDPR statement in the footer of the CV? | **Yes** | No |

# Video CVs

Video CVs are used a lot in creative roles in marketing and media. You can have a go at producing one if it is going to be useful to you. Smith (2023) discusses some ways to produce and deliver a video CV. Video CVs should be used to supplement a written application. They can be uploaded to a video hosting site or sent directly to the employer as a video file. The running time should be kept to a minimum, usually between one and three minutes. Smith (2023) offers some pros and cons:

Video CV pros:

- helps you stand out from the crowd – by going the extra mile
- showcases your creativity – in doing your own thing
- displays your personality – creating a memorable impact
- demonstrates particular skills – such as public speaking

Video CV cons:

- standing out for the wrong reasons – highlighting flaws such as shyness
- selling yourself short – time constraints prevent you from including relevant details
- time-consuming production – your time could be spent perfecting the application instead
- irritating your prospective employer – they might consider it a hassle to load and view the video

Other things you will need to consider are whether you have access to suitable technical requirements such as good-quality video and audio recording, lighting and editing software. You will also need to be well rehearsed and word-perfect when speaking to camera. Hesitancy or waffle can be off-putting to the viewer. Look online for examples of video CVs, contact your career advisors for advice or seek out alumni/mentors who have experience in producing video CVs.

# Cover Letter/Email

Besides your CV, you also need to gain experience in producing a cover letter. These are usually produced in the form of a short, introductory email, or as an attachment to an email as a Word document or PDF. Check the job application to see what the employer prefers or specifies.

## Hear from the Expert

"We get lots of applications. The main thing I look for in a cover letter is for somebody to have clearly read what we're advertising. If it is not clear which role people are applying for that can be confusing and we want people to be really interested in the role that we are offering. If you've read the description and done a bit of research, you can outline the skills that you are going to bring to the role."

*– Megan Shore, Programmes Manager, Ignite!*

The cover email will introduce yourself, explain why you are the right person for the job you are applying for, and give a brief explanation of your relevant skills. As with the CV, you can create a draft version of a cover email, but you will need to tailor it for specific jobs. Use simple, straightforward language. Don't be overly formal or, at the other extreme, too casual. If you have researched the organisation you are applying to, you should be able to gauge what type of language or register is appropriate. Try to avoid using superlatives or clichés such as 'extremely' or 'I am a people-person'. The cover email should be kept short and concise (three or four short paragraphs), reflecting the style and design of your CV.

## Hear from the Experts

"A cover letter that is really specific will definitely make me interested in having a call with them. Spell checking is important. Sometimes we get cover letters and CVs that have got mistakes in and that's just not very good practice. An employer would hope that an applicant has had a proper look at what they're sending before they send it. It reflects a level of professionalism."

*– Megan Shore, Programmes Manager, Ignite!*

"In general, the creative industry isn't all that professional. I'm not saying you should swear in an email, but you can put some emojis in there, you can make a joke or two, or say something that might sound a bit cringy. I definitely do that, and for me that really led to a lot of responses quite quickly. I was made redundant towards the end of last year, so I re-experienced the scramble to get a job quickly, which you will probably feel after graduation. And in that time I got the most responses by really sitting and thinking about what is going to go in that email to make me sound friendly and like an actual person. Compliment their work, talk about your work and what you're passionate about. That's definitely led to me having more chats with people instead of being ignored."

*– Em Green, Motion Designer, Alive With Ideas*

"My best piece of advice for when you're applying for jobs would be when writing a cover letter, avoid doing the standard thing. Don't just say, 'oh, I'm organised and a fast learner' and things like that. Those are great, but people want to know more than that. Try and make it a bit different. Make yourself stand out. When I applied for my job with DeCantillon Films, I thought, you know, I'm going to push the boat out. I wrote in the cover letter about why *Star Trek: Beyond* flopped in the box office, and why they should have played with the fact that it was the 50th anniversary of *Star Trek* the same year *Star Trek: Beyond* was being released. They should have used that to their advantage in the film's marketing campaign and they, for whatever reason, did not. That part of the cover letter is apparently why one of the producers recruited me. He said, 'I mean, you've got the job, as soon as we read that we were like, yeah, this is why we want her'. So be creative and push the boat out."

*– Laura Savage, Marketing Director, DeCantillon Films*

## Exercise: Producing Your Cover Letter/Email

Now you have produced your CV, you should write your **cover letter**/email. Look back at the job you identified and tailored your CV to suit and do the same with your cover letter/email.

Remember to follow the guidelines we set out above and organise the content in the following structure:

- Addressing the cover letter/email – having researched the organisation (through the internet and LinkedIn), you should address the email to the person you know will be reading it. Addressing it to a named person will impress the recipient as it is evidence of your research and networking skills
- Paragraph 1 – introduce yourself and the job role you are applying for. You can also mention here where you saw the job advertised
- Paragraph 2 – write about your relevant experience. You should refer to the keywords mentioned in the job advert here, as doing so will align your experience directly with the role
- Paragraph 3 – highlight your suitability for the job and why you are interested in working for the organisation, and what you can offer them. This is where you will need to have done some research to tailor the application to the job advert
- Paragraph 4 – summarise your interest in the job and your keenness for an interview
- Sign off with 'yours sincerely' (if you have addressed a named person at the start of the cover letter/email) or 'yours faithfully' (if you have not been able to find the recipient's name)
- Lastly, and importantly, check your spelling and grammar!

As with the CV that you produced in the earlier exercise, it is a good idea to ask one of your peers, or a reliable friend or mentor, to review your cover letter/email. Remember to show them a copy of the job advert before they read your cover letter/email. Once you receive their feedback, redraft the cover email as needed. You can also make an appointment with your university's careers advisor and ask them to have a look at your CV and cover letter/email.

**Student Voice**

"Don't leave applications too late. Rushing an application will mean you may miss mistakes on your CV or cover letter and won't make a good first impression on your placement provider. Instead, dedicate an hour to go over a prospective application and get someone to proof-read it before you submit it."

*– Emily May Drummond, Media Production student*

**Hear from the Experts**

"From my experience the number of times that someone sends an email via the station or the company website and it's just a generic email. You would immediately go it's a no because [they have taken no] effort ... to work out who the person is, what their name is and what their email address. All that information is available, you should be able to find that out. Also, it's very easy to cut and paste but don't do that because I have had emails addressed in my email address with someone else's name throughout them!"

*– Dick Stone, Broadcast Consultant*

"If you're thinking about directly contacting an editor of a radio station or TV channel, don't write a generic 'Dear Sir or Madam' and especially don't just put 'Sir' because if a woman is the editor, you won't make the best impression. Go that extra mile to find out their name and address the email to them. It's not hard to find out that information."

*– Emma Snow, Journalist, BBC*

# Conclusion

In this chapter we have enabled you to give a focused look at developing and targeting your CV. You now understand how to format a CV and how to tailor it to specific jobs. Similarly, the exercise you have carried out in writing a cover letter/email will also help you to follow a set of simple guidelines to create a good first impression to prospective employers. Taking this approach will demonstrate that you are the person they are looking to recruit.

The next set of career materials that will arm you in your search for work experience is the topic of the next chapter. We will look at professional branding, social media and creating an online portfolio.

## Further Reading

You can find further useful information on building your CV, writing your cover letter/ email and creating your video CVs, including some examples, on the following websites:

creativetoolkit.org.uk

Prospects.ac.uk

tvwatercooler.org

Other useful sources include:

Becker, Lucinda (2020) *Write a Brilliant CV*. London: Sage. This book is a 'quick skills' guide to producing a persuasive, targeted CV.

Mills, Corinne (2015) *You're Hired! CV: How to Write a Brilliant CV*. Bath: Trotman Indigo Publishing. This is a step-by-step guide to help you turn a record of your experience into a carefully crafted CV.

Ricketts, Gavin (2012) *TV Runner Handbook and CV Template*. London: Napoleon Creative Books. This book is specifically for those wanting to break into television. It includes a detailed template to help you write a CV when applying for your first job in TV or film, as a runner or production assistant.

Smith, Jemma (2023, May) 'Create a great video CV'. *Prospects* [website]. www.prospects.ac.uk/careers-advice/cvs-and-cover-letters/create-a-great-video-cv. This article provides some detailed advice about creating a video CV, including the preparation, filming and technical aspects to consider.

# 8

# BUILDING YOUR BRAND FOR WORK EXPERIENCE

## Managing Your Digital Footprint

## Introduction

In the previous chapter we started taking some practical steps in preparing you for your applications for work experience by helping you with writing a CV. In this chapter we are going to start by helping you to build on your personal brand. We will look at networking strategies, examining your **digital footprint** and developing a bank of materials that will professionalise your brand further.

The aims and outcomes for this chapter are:

* to carry out an analysis of your online presence and how you present yourself
* to conduct a 'social media makeover'
* to develop the materials that sell your professional brand

List of exercises in this chapter

* Analysing your digital footprint
* Analysing a professional online profile
* Building your professional profile/brand
* Analysing your portfolio

Having a personal 'brand' has become something of a buzzword in recent years, intensified by the use of social media. The term is often emphasised by influencers and vloggers who depend on selling their personality to make a living. However, it can be useful for anybody and is not exclusive to this type of employment. Having a brand is about the way you construct an image of yourself; it can therefore be a very useful way of presenting yourself to potential employers.

─┤ **Hear from the Experts** ├──────────────────────────────

"If you have a pre-existing brand, or if you're trying to create a new one, try to be original. It may be very hard because a lot of things have been done before, but just be true to who you are. Add that flair of professionalism to your brand, because otherwise it may be hard for others to take you seriously. Creating original and professional branding is always a really good way to make that first impression and gain connections."

*– Shakirah Jelley, Digital Content Creator*

"Show off the skills and things that you have done at university, whether they are projects or extracurricular. Showing that you have these skills and – I hate to say it – showing what sets you apart from the crowd, that's exactly what you have to do. You have to be able to show why you're a unique person, what your experience is and where you come from. Jobwise, it's ultimately about you being open about who you are and what you're looking for which is important."

*– Louis Nunn, Marketing Coordinator, Freeths LLP*

"You can be that little bit more unique and quirkier out there because that's what media creators are looking for. They're looking for enthusiastic, passionate people who are creative and critically minded. You're not going to get that with someone who's really boring and black and white, so it's OK to have a little bit of a 'pop' in your personality, and branding can bring that out of you."

*– Shakirah Jelley, Digital Content Creator*

# Your Existing Digital Footprint

You have probably read news stories about celebrities or sports stars who have had their careers threatened by online content which has come back to haunt them. In terms of your own social media presence, posing with a cocktail on a night out might be appropriate on a personal online profile, but it may not present a professional image to an employer or placement provider. It is increasingly common for employers to do an online search for any content about potential employees. With this in mind, let's consider for a moment how you already present yourself to the world via social media. We will do this with the following exercise.

## Exercise: Analysing Your Digital Footprint

You can perform this task yourself, or you can work with another student and give them permission to search for you online. They should search under your name and also do an image search.

Once the results have been found, complete a 'digital footprint' analysis by noting down:

- where online content about yourself was found (Facebook, Twitter/X, TikTok, Instagram, YouTube for example)
- a description of the online content that was found about yourself (for example, holiday snaps, selfies, or A-Level projects)
- the impression your online content will present to potential employers. *Be honest about this!*

Reflect on this exercise and consider how you might reorganise your online identity. Is there anything potentially embarrassing or distasteful about what has been found? Are you 'oversharing'? Would it be appropriate to alter the privacy settings on some of your accounts, for example by deleting old accounts that you don't use anymore and hiding/locking accounts that are more personal?

It is worth pointing out here that this exercise can work both ways. Before applying for work with a potential employer or organisation, you can look at the way they present themselves to the public. It may give you clues about the way they would expect you to present yourself to them.

## Exercise: Analysing a Professional Online Profile

This exercise will help you to see how professionals in your field present themselves online. Search and view the profiles of people in a career area you aspire to. It could be the person you interviewed for the case study in Chapter 4. Analyse their professional brand by undertaking the following tasks:

- Note down the tools and media they use to put across their professional brand. There may be a LinkedIn profile, a website/portfolio, social media sites like Twitter/X, Facebook, Instagram, TikTok, YouTube, Vimeo, or a blog
- List the features of their brand that you like and might use to develop your own brand. For example, you might focus on:
  - their profile photo and any other images used
  - their profile information, such as a mini biography
  - the summary of their career to date
  - information about their employment history and work experience
  - their listing of the career-specific skills they offer
  - any recommendations and endorsements they include
  - their connections and networks
  - the groups and companies they follow
- Did looking at this professional profile encourage you to use a broad range of online applications in your own branding? How do the organisations you have looked at model their content to appear professional and did you learn anything from this? Make a note of your thoughts. Can you use this exercise to contribute

to developing your own professional network, such as by following the same groups, companies and connections?

- Compile a list of tips and hints, based on the above criteria, that will help you to develop your own professional branding as we progress through this chapter

# Tools for Building a Professional Brand

The two exercises above have helped you to think about how your digital footprint can be considered in the context of employability. Now you have analysed your own digital footprint and the online profiles of professionals, it is time to start building your own profile or brand. There are many platforms and applications available to help you build your brand. We are going to outline these below so you can make a choice about which to use for an exercise later in the chapter.

## LinkedIn

This platform is a networking site specifically designed for showcasing your skills, qualifications and experience, and for connecting with likeminded peers and potential employers. It is a useful site to use in building your brand because there is a clear division between the 'professional' profiles on this site and other platforms that can be used for more social purposes. An added bonus is that if you are signed up to LinkedIn you can gain specialist qualifications via LinkedIn Learning, a vast series of online modules. Certificates passed on these courses can be added to your profile.

### Student Voice

"My advice to students would be to never underestimate the power of LinkedIn. There are many great individuals on there who are happy to provide information and give opportunities to enthusiastic jobseekers. Use LinkedIn, connect, network and reach out to those people within industries that you wish to pursue a career in. The worst you will get is no response!"

– *Michael Goulding, Graduate Development Programme student*

## Portfolio/Website

You might think about developing a professional portfolio in the form of web pages using a web-building application. The bonus with this is that you can bring several aspects of content together, such as writing, photography and video, all to one site. There are several positive reasons why you should create a portfolio, and these are:

- to stand out from the crowd
- to show evidence of your creativity
- to show how good you are at your work
- to help set an agenda for your job interviews

It should be immediately clear to the viewer what your specialism is and what you are 'selling'. Are you showcasing design skills (for example, in costume, or hair and make-up)? Are you showcasing videography skills in the form of short clips or showreels? Or are you showcasing your music with video clips and audio files? Photographic, video and audio content should include a short piece of writing (for example, a brief caption or sentence) to explain what it is. You might also want to briefly say how you created the work (for example, naming the software or application).

You can preview your web pages for different devices to make sure you are happy with its visual impact and design. (Web-building and blog sites often have a preview facility to test what the layout will look like on desktops, tablets and phones).

## Student Voice

"When I was entering the media production industry, having a professional portfolio was essential. In many application stages for jobs, sending off a portfolio of work, in my case a media production showreel, was an essential aspect of applying. Companies are interested in the work you have completed throughout university, freelance work or any other opportunities to see in which areas of production your skills are and/or where they can be developed. My first job out of university was working as a Digital Media Executive for a company within the automotive industry – working on all things social media, photography, videography and website development. During the application stage for this role, I was asked out of the blue to provide a showreel, demonstrating various projects within production I had been involved in. Thankfully, I had always ensured to keep an up-to-date portfolio of all production work!"

*– Michael Goulding, Graduate Development Programme student*

## Video Sharing

You can develop your professional brand via video-sharing sites such as YouTube, Vimeo and TikTok. You can also embed or share the content to other sites, such as your blog, Twitter/X or Facebook. You should be selective about showcasing your best and most appropriate work.

─┤ **Hear from the Expert** ├────────────────────────────────

"Video is obviously pivotal to what I do, being a videographer, but as a creative in general I think that it's incredibly important to share your work. It enables you to build an audience and network of those that resonate with your stuff. Video itself is an especially captivating medium but it's also important to use it in the right way. Not everything needs motion – sometimes strong photography is all that is needed to elevate a post."

*– Jacob Germany, Videographer*

─── **Student Voice** ───────────────────────────────────

"At the moment, I have yet to consistently and effectively use video sharing/streaming platforms to support my professional brand. I primarily use YouTube as a way to share unlisted drafts and completed audio-visual projects (for viewing purposes) to contributors and employers. This is because there are a lot less complications that can arise compared to cloud sharing sites. YouTube is very user friendly to enable less tech savvy individuals to easily view the work."

*– Callum Roome, postgraduate Media student*

## Blogging

Blogging might be your choice of sharing your brand and creating your professional profile. Blogging platforms can be particularly useful for showcasing your writing skills. Creating regular and up-to-date content can be time-consuming, so you are best advised to keep the word count brief and concise if you can. It is best to focus on a particular and relevant theme that demonstrates your knowledge and expertise in a particular area.

## Vlogging

Vlogging has become a very popular way of creating a professional brand. As with blogging, it is best to find a particular theme or niche to focus on to give your vlog some consistency. Vlogging can be useful if you want to show off presenting or public-speaking skills. Vlogs can also demonstrate your skills in camerawork, lighting, set dressing and editing. The downside to vlogging is that it can highlight flaws if you are not very skilled at being on camera. You need to have an engaging personality to carry it off.

## ScreenSkills

You can sign up and create a profile on the screenskills.com website, which offers support for creatives working in the media and creative industries. Similarly to LinkedIn, this site also has some specialist training modules to enhance your experience. Being able to demonstrate these skills can be seen as a bonus to your future employers.

## Internet Movie Database (IMDb) and FilmFreeway

You can sign up to and explore the IMDb database (imdb.com). Filmmakers who have an account can list their work on IMDb after it has been approved for posting on the site. Usually, you have to provide evidence that your work has been premiered somewhere, for example, at a festival. You can also use it for writing reviews, networking and finding out about the film and TV sector.

FilmFreeway (filmfreeway.com) is a useful site for collating the promotional materials you create prior to entering films and screenplays into festivals and contests. After signing up and creating an account, you can upload video content, synopses, promotional photos and posters to the site. FilmFreeway also allows you to find relevant or appropriate festivals, including those that are free to enter, by using search filters. You can also use these filters to narrow your search, for example, to find LGBTQ+ festivals or contests for films produced by diverse production teams. Use the site to store all your video files and promotional material and revisit it regularly to keep your festival entries up to date.

### Student Voice

"I have used FilmFreeway to promote and enter projects into film festivals. The one tip that I would give to people who want to do the same is to make sure you prepare film festival materials (e.g. poster, trailer, still, director bio, etc.) in advance and make sure to make these as high quality as the film you are submitting. Based on my own experiences, I would definitely suggest finding help or contracting someone to make your poster if graphic design is not your strong suit. I would also suggest keeping your projects up to date by adding any laurels you receive to your posters and trailers. As I was told recently by an established filmmaker, laurels help to give credibility to your work and are an eye catcher for potential festivals and employers/clients. You worked hard to win those laurels, so display them proudly!"

– *Callum Roome, postgraduate Media student*

## Other Social Media

You can develop, improve on or create a professional social media account using a social media platform, such as:

- Behance (behance.net) – is a creative network for showcasing work in a wide range of creative areas and connecting with other people and their work
- CREATEBritain (createbritain.com) – is a directory and resource for creative people to network and showcase their work

- The Dots (the-dots.com) – is a social media platform for creatives and freelancers to share their work, to network and to find jobs and work experience opportunities
- Instagram – is particularly useful if you want to showcase photographic or other visual work
- Twitter/X and Facebook – are useful for showcasing, sharing work and networking

If you already have personal social media sites using any of the above platforms, consider creating a separate one purely for professional purposes. This will help you to avoid mixing the personal and the professional.

## Hear from the Experts

"The big thing I really want to get across is to be human, to actually come across like a human being to these people. It's great to send emails and contact people. But if you sound like a robot, they're not going to read it and they're not going to bother to look at your work. So try and sound real, try and put personality into everything that you do, whether that's a portfolio website or a Behance page, but especially in the emails that you're writing to people."

*– Em Green, Motion Designer, Alive With Ideas*

"The advice that I can give you is to support yourself by creating a professional platform on LinkedIn, a website and other platforms. Your social media is where employers like ourselves go to view your work, experience and journey. Having an online presence is going to be key so make this count and keep this professional, as it reflects on your reputation and what you can offer an employer and company."

*– Radha Singh, CEO/Creative Director, THE HOUSE OF RADHA*

"LinkedIn, Instagram, TikTok, YouTube – it depends which audience you're trying to reach with your work. The big one for me at the moment is Instagram because the majority of users are millennial, which is the target market for the agency that I work in. The best site for building a personal brand is 100% LinkedIn, though – most of my recruitment opportunities have come through posting regularly on there."

*– Jacob Germany, Videographer*

"CREATEBritain is a new online platform for finding and promoting everyone and everything in the creative industry. People find you because you've got the relevant skills that they're looking for and everyone has an equal opportunity to come at the top of search results."

*– Richard Woods, Co-founder, CREATEBritain.com*

"Something I have learned is the importance of controlling my digital footprint by utilising professional social media accounts to their fullest (e.g. LinkedIn, Instagram, Twitter/X, and even my own website). Expanding contacts, promoting and remaining active on these accounts will keep potential employers or clients up to date on my career developments, as well as showcasing my skills. This could be as simple as posting updates on current projects; attending a work event or training; or promoting completed pieces or achievements. All will help develop a professional image online."

*– Callum Roome, postgraduate Media student*

# Building Your Professional Profile/Brand

## Exercise: Building Your Professional Profile/Brand

For this exercise we suggest that you focus on either building a LinkedIn profile or a professional online portfolio. Do some work on developing one of these, using the advice given below.

## Advice on Setting up Your Linkedin Profile

A good LinkedIn profile will include:

- a short headline that contains key words about you and what you have to offer
- a professional-looking head shot that aligns with your career ambition – you can ask a friend to take a photo specifically for this site rather than using a pre-existing photo, such as a selfie
- a summary profile/mini biography which indicates the career area you are in or one you are interested in, some unique selling points, and an indication of whether you are looking for work
- place/s of education – as an undergraduate you can list the institution and course you are currently studying at
- education and training – this can include any qualifications and professional courses you have passed, such as health and safety, or technical training or LinkedIn Learning modules
- extra-curricular – this can include membership of student societies, travel and wider interests
- experience – information about work experience (both paid and voluntary); include links to the websites of any organisations you have worked with
- employment – include part-time work during studies and identify the transferable skills you have gained

- projects – links to projects you have completed at university, such as relevant **client-led** projects
- a collection of career skills to be endorsed by employers
- written recommendations from employers or work experience providers
- evidence of linking with news feeds and other relevant professional content
- professional associations/groups/your professional network – for example, linking with companies you are interested in or a link to your alumni association

Go to LinkedIn.com to find out more information and to set up an account. Your university careers service may also run workshops to assist and advise you on setting up a LinkedIn profile and account.

## Advice on Setting up Your Online Portfolio

You can design a personal website either by buying a personalised domain name or by using a free app such as Wix, WordPress or Squarespace.

A good online portfolio will include:

- a menu of the contents – including a navigation bar and links
- a profile/personal statement – including key achievements, accomplishments and personal qualities
- a professional mission statement – a short statement on what drives you
- some key achievements and accomplishments – how they relate to the work you are looking for
- key skills – your top skills and evidence of where you have used them
- career summary/goals – a description of your work ethic and work interests, including an idea of where you see yourself being in 2–5 years' time
- CV – including a downloadable one as a PDF and also one that displays on screen
- a sample of your best work relevant to your career area – for example, images, videos, social media content, samples of your writing and reports (include no more than 10 samples which provide variety)
- **testimonials**/letters of recommendation – a collection of any positive comments about you received from customers, clients, colleagues and past employers, and feedback from work experience providers. You can also include articles about you and your work
- examples of volunteering – especially where the skills developed are relevant to your career
- certificates, lists of relevant awards and university transcripts, courses and training attended – these can include LinkedIn Learning and ScreenSkills modules and courses
- a contact page with details about how potential employers can reach you – this can include links to LinkedIn, social media profiles and video-sharing sites

Here are some tips and hints to help you:

*   make sure the portfolio is of consistent style and design by keeping the font style, size and colours simple, and achieving a balance between text and images. Use an accessibility checker to ensure a good level of readability for a diverse audience
*   ensure the pages and links are easy to navigate and follow
*   ensure that any images, videos and audio files have explanatory captions, and state their length and duration
*   if using examples from group work, identify your role. Include appropriate acknowledgements, permissions and copyright information
*   for each sample of work, provide some context – a brief description, the process for the work and the challenges you overcame
*   proof-read it!

## Hear from the Experts

"If you want to work in motion design or animation or digital design, I would definitely say when it comes to portfolios, have a website that you have designed. It shows that you've put that effort in. But don't make it static – I made this mistake in the beginning. I had a website that was just full of static thumbnails of projects that were animated. But it doesn't show the work all that well, to just use static images. So now my homepage has little gifs of a few seconds of animation from each of those projects. Let them see that it moves. I think this applies to graphic design and digital design as well. If you've done a branding project that has lots of outcomes and applications, have a set of still images that just cycles through. Put that on your home page, show the whole project easily, put it in front of their face because people don't have time to be clicking on loads of different things to look at a whole project. That's really important."

*– Em Green, Motion Designer, Alive With Ideas*

"I advise you start putting together a portfolio of all of your work. I have a hard drive containing all my work – my practical projects, scripts, documentaries, and podcasts that I've been work-ing on. Whether that's stuff that I've been doing on my course or work placements, or even personal projects. It's a good idea to collate them all."

*– Sam Reynolds, Video and Motion Producer*

## Exercise: Analysing Your Portfolio

Once you have completed a draft of your portfolio it is time to analyse it for quality. You can perform this exercise yourself. However, it is much better to pair up with one of your peers and allow them to analyse your portfolio while you analyse theirs. Even better, see if you can run your portfolio past a mentor, or someone you have identified in your career case study in Chapter 4. Enlist the help of someone who has a keen eye and who will give you an honest opinion. Their feedback can help you to produce an outstanding portfolio rather than one that is merely 'good'.

Provide the reviewer with the **career portfolio** evaluation form below. Judgement should be based on initial impact, but also on attention to detail (checking for typos and spelling mistakes). Ask your reviewer to use the evaluation form, ticking the 'yes' or 'no' columns and making constructive suggestions for improvement in the final column.

Once you are happy that your portfolio is completed to your full satisfaction, having taken into account the feedback from your reviewer/s, then it is ready to publish.

| Question | Yes | No | Comments and suggestions |
|---|---|---|---|
| **Impact/Design/Navigation** | | | |
| Does the portfolio look professional and inviting on first viewing? | | | |
| Is the URL appropriate/short enough? | | | |
| Does the weblink work? | | | |
| Is the navigation simple and clear? | | | |
| Is the typography and design simple and appropriate? | | | |
| **Home/About/Profile page** | | | |
| Is the head shot appropriate and professional? | | | |
| Is there a clear sense of a career aspiration? | | | |
| Is there a sense of professional branding? | | | |
| Are there links to professional social media? | | | |
| Are all the social media links professional rather than personal? | | | |
| Does the profile page make appropriate use of bold, colour and italic text? | | | |
| Does the profile page use bulleted lists to highlight important points? | | | |
| Are there any typos or spelling mistakes? | | | |
| **CV (Curriculum Vitae)** | | | |
| Is there a link to a CV? | | | |
| Is the CV a maximum of two pages long? | | | |

*(Continued)*

| Question | Yes | No | Comments and suggestions |
|---|---|---|---|
| Is the CV downloadable as a printable PDF as well as displayed on screen? | | | |
| Does the CV have name and contact details on it? | | | |
| **Examples of work** | | | |
| Are examples of work shown in the portfolio, e.g. videos, photos and projects? | | | |
| Is there a clear explanation of what work is being shown and why? | | | |
| Is there an explanation of what role the author of the profile took in producing the examples of work, especially if it was a group project? | | | |
| **Contact page** | | | |
| Are there links on the contacts page to professional social media? | | | |
| Is it clear for readers how they can make contact? | | | |
| **Testimonials/Recommendations** | | | |
| Are the testimonials/recommendations from an appropriate source and are they named? | | | |

# Conclusion

This chapter has helped you to develop or improve your professional brand. By analysing your digital footprint, you have been able to consider the impression that placement providers and future employers might have of you. You have been encouraged to perform a 'social media makeover' to ensure a professional image of yourself. We have also provided an overview of the types of platforms you can consider using to showcase your work. The exercises have encouraged you to develop a LinkedIn profile or an online portfolio.

In the next chapter we will focus on searching for work experience, making applications and being interviewed for a work experience placement.

# Further Reading

Beverland, Michael (2021) *Brand Management: Co-creating Meaningful Brands*. London: Sage. This book is a theoretical and practical guide to brands. Although it uses case studies from major brands, some of the principles in its chapters on brand consistency and creating new brands may be useful for your research into self-branding.

Hennessey, Brittany (2018) *Influencer: Building Your Personal Brand in the Age of Social Media*. New York: Citadel Press. This book is a guide to core influencer principles and may help you in building an online brand.

Marwick, Alice (2015) *Status Update: Celebrity, Publicity, and Branding in the Social Media Age*. New Haven, CT: Yale University Press. This book provides an analysis of publicity and branding via social media. Chapter 4 on self-branding may be of particular interest.

# 9

# SECURING YOUR PLACEMENT

## Applying and Interviewing for Work Experience

## Introduction

In the previous chapter we did some attentive work on developing your digital footprint and professional brand. This chapter focuses on honing the skills you will need to set up and apply for a placement. We will focus on searching for work experience, making applications and being interviewed for a work experience placement. The chapter also includes some tips and hints on how to look after your wellbeing while applying and preparing for interviews for a placement.

The aims and outcomes for this chapter are:

- to find out about applying for placements
- to offer guidance and support on being interviewed for placements
- to prepare for and undertake a practice/mock interview that you can reflect on for the future
- to help you set up a placement
- to develop the art of pitching for self-employment
- to support your wellbeing while securing a placement

List of exercises in this chapter:

- Using a placement search checklist form
- Answering competency-based questions using the STAR(R) technique
- Preparing an elevator pitch

# Conducting a Placement Search

In Chapter 6 we gave some pointers as to where you might find some work experience. We will now shift the focus to searching for and securing a placement in the media and creative industries. Here are some tips and hints to assist you in your placement search:

- remind yourself of what you want to achieve from a placement – relate back to Chapter 6 where you identified your SMART objectives for work experience
- undertake your search – make sure you look at a wide variety of possible sources for placements
- do your research – align your search for placements with your skills and experience. Research the organisations thoroughly to ensure they match your requirements
- be tenacious in your search – accept that you will probably have to apply for a lot, and you will not necessarily be successful first time. See rejection as a learning opportunity
- get your application materials in order – tailor your CV, cover email, portfolio and social media profiles to suit the sorts of placements you are applying for
- be proactive in your search – don't be afraid to follow up your applications with a phone call to enquire about the role and to ask for further details. This will help you make an impression and demonstrate your confidence

## Student Voice

"Before you start your search, ask yourself what you want to achieve during that placement, whether that be a personal goal, or developing technical or networking skills. Having a clear goal in mind can be really helpful in picking out a placement because it gets you thinking about what type of placement will help you achieve it."

*– Emily May Drummond, Media Production student*

# Creating Your Own Placement

One of the suggestions we made in Chapter 6 was that you can create your own placement rather than applying in response to an advert. Creating your own placement will involve identifying and contacting an employer that you would really like to work with and negotiating an opportunity with them. There are two possible ways to do this. The first is by negotiating a specific role for yourself within the organisation; the second is to negotiate a brief for a project or body of work that you can undertake on their behalf.

## Negotiating a Role

Let us start by looking at how to negotiate a role for your placement:

- first, identify the organisation you are interested in negotiating a placement with and find the contact details of a named person to whom to address your proposal

- consider what your proposal is. Suggest a job title and role, and provide brief job description (refer back to Chapter 4 where we looked at examples of job adverts for help with this)
- consider what you can offer the employer in terms of skills, personal qualities, qualifications and experience. It is important to be able to demonstrate what you can offer them, not just what they can offer you
- identify what you would like to get out of the proposed placement (refer back to your SMART objectives in Chapter 6)

The process of negotiating the role will also require you to:

- consider the length of the placement (dates and hours), the location (on site, remote, or hybrid) and the type of supervision required (for example, regular meetings and updates with the employer)
- provide evidence of your skills and experience through your CV, portfolio, social media and examples of your work
- negotiate links with your university if it is an assessed part of your degree course. For example, by putting the organisation in contact with your tutor or careers department, asking them to provide a reference for you at the end of the placement, and satisfying the necessary health and safety requirements

## Student Voices

"Don't wait for opportunities to find you – be proactive and find opportunities which interest you. These don't always have to be advertised or available. Be confident to contact individuals or companies, asking whether it would be possible to provide a desired opportunity."

*– Nikolas Sklinidjis, Media Production student*

"Use any resources and people you know to attempt to find work. Make use of media-specific job-hunting sites such as 'The TV Watercooler' and 'The Talent Manager'. I can also recommend Facebook groups such as 'People in TV'. These sites and groups are extremely helpful."

*– Liv Louis, Freelance Production Runner/Media Production student*

"Don't be shy – feel comfortable asking for things which will benefit you, such as availability or role expectations. This can be the difference between finding an opportunity and a beneficial and valuable opportunity."

*– Nikolas Sklinidjis, Media Production student*

"Search for production companies which are based in your desired area of work. If there's a contact email or telephone number, don't be afraid to mail or call and ask if they would be willing to take on someone for experience! Moreover, I found that production companies were more than happy to accommodate someone on placement for a week or so. Everybody has to start somewhere and these people understand that. Most people love to have people with a keen interest in their job learn from them!"

*– Liv Louis, Freelance Production Runner/Media Production student*

"My tips for students sourcing a placement are to start thinking early about what sort of work placement you want to do, so that you know which role to apply for. Attend career fairs and other events related to careers to get ideas about what you want to do and meet new people."

*– Kennis Tang, Media Production student*

## Negotiating a Brief for a Project

The second way of creating your own placement is to negotiate a brief for a project with a potential employer. For example, this could be producing a short video or social media content for a small company or charity, which might not otherwise be able to support a formal placement. Negotiating the project will entail the following:

*   identify the organisation you are interested in negotiating a project with and find the contact details of a named person to whom to address your proposal
*   consider what the product of the project will be (a video, podcast, social media posts or a report, for example) and how this will be realised
*   consider what you can offer the employer in terms of the skills and qualities you have and provide evidence of these

Completing the form below will help you with your negotiations.

---

**Proposed Project Briefing**

Your name and contact details

Employer contact details

University contact details (if appropriate)

**Project Briefing**

Media form, e.g. a video, a photo exhibition, an audio piece, website, social media content

Proposed content/subject of the project

Proposed treatment – how you intend to approach the subject of the project

Length/size of the product

Main aims for the project

Audience and market

Deadline for completion

Schedule/timeline, including deadline for the project

Any other issues, e.g. consideration of health and safety, safeguarding, locations and logistics

Examples of previous projects or similar products available on the market

---

## Reaching an Agreement for the Proposed Placement

Whether you are negotiating a placement role or a placement project it is important to reach a formal agreement on the terms of the placement with the employer. This agreement should cover the following:

- shared expectations – have you agreed on the outcome of the placement for each of the stakeholders: the employer, your course (if appropriate) and yourself?
- realistic and achievable goals – have you established how the placement will fit with your lifestyle, course timetable and other commitments?
- the timeline, schedule, deadline, completion of the placement/project – are the parameters of the placement/project clearly defined? Have you agreed to a formal sign-off date?
- access to production facilities and resources – will you be using university equipment and resources, your own, or will these be provided by the employer?
- budget considerations – has the responsibility for any costs been agreed? (Costs include the payment of expenses or renumeration, a budget for resources and materials, and provision for travel and subsistence)
- copyright and intellectual property rights – if you have produced a body of work for the employer, is it clear who this belongs to and the terms of its use?
- receiving feedback – do you have an agreement on the provision of a reference or recommendation on completion of the work?

Your agreement should show attention to detail and be written down and signed, where appropriate. If the placement is part of your course, you are advised to share and seek advice on this agreement with your course tutor and/or careers department to keep them informed of your progress. It is important to keep in contact with university staff for reasons of health and safety too.

Now that we have looked at how to search for a placement and how to create your own, we will turn our attention to conducting your search and administrating it.

# Administration of Your Placement Search

No doubt you will be applying for several placement opportunities at the same time. The golden rule for your placement search is to be organised and manage it well. Doing so will help you to avoid some common pitfalls experienced by students, such as:

- double-booking placements – mismanaging your calendar
- missing opportunities – not keeping an eye on your emails
- taking on too much – prioritising quantity over quality
- over-committing – offering too much

## Student Voices

"A key scenario to avoid would be over-committing to one opportunity. Even if an opportunity looks perfect to you, keep your options open as you never know when something will fall through. Try to look out for key signs, such as poor reply times, which may be a sign that an opportunity might not materialise as expected. Multiple options allow you to decide which works best for you and which will be the best experience."

– Nikolas Sklinidjis, Media Production student

"Don't get stuck in your comfort zone. The whole point of a placement is to get you experiencing new things, so trying to challenge yourself by choosing something that you've not done before will mean that you get the most out of the experience. Even if you don't enjoy it, you might find that you've gained interpersonal skills instead, which is still a form of development!"

*– Emily May Drummond, Media Production student*

You can create your own simple form for record-keeping while searching for a placement. The following exercise will help you to do this.

## Exercise: Using a Placement Search Checklist Form

You should duplicate and complete the form below for each of the placements you are applying for. Refer to the job adverts and fill in each detail appropriate for your search in the middle column. Use the notes/comments section to keep a record of any extra details, such as whether you need to tailor your CV, and when to practise your interview techniques, for instance.

| Action | Detail | Notes/comments |
|---|---|---|
| Employer/organisation | | |
| Job title | | |
| Role (job description, duties and responsibilities) | | |
| Skills and experience required | | |
| Person specification (the attributes required of the ideal candidate) | | |
| Outline of basic research on the organisation (e.g. details of ethos, customers and audience) | | |
| Name of contact and their job title | | |
| Email/phone number | | |
| Website link and social media | | |
| Address/location of the organisation | | |
| Where the placement was advertised | | |
| Start date | | |
| Total number of hours for the placement | | |
| Expected number of hours per week | | |
| Application deadline | | |
| Application materials required (e.g. CV, cover email, portfolio, online application form) | | |
| Interview details (e.g. individual interview, group interview, online interview, phone interview) | | |
| Interview date | | |

# Make a Speculative Application

Making a speculative application involves approaching a potential placement provider to ask if there is work available even if an opportunity has not been advertised. A first step might be to email and attach a copy of your CV. Be aware, however, that organisations might receive a large number of emails every day and your message may be overlooked. Two of the best ways to stand out in these circumstances are to address your email to a named person that you have found through researching the organisation, and then to follow up your email with a phone call. You can make the call one or two weeks after sending the email. There is further information about targeting CVs and writing cover emails in Chapter 7.

Remember to tailor your application materials to suit the placement you are applying for and be ready to be persistent. Remember, too, that everyone receives a number of rejections until something positive turns up.

## Hear from the Expert

"Do your research and find out about the company. Find out what makes the business different to its competitors and mention some of those things in your application because as the employer, we want to feel loved. We want to feel like you really want to work for us. By taking the time to research the business, tailoring your approach and showcasing that background knowledge in your application, I am more likely to remember you, offer you an interview and hopefully give you an opportunity either now or in the future."

*– Tom Walters, Managing Director, The Dairy*

## Student Voices

"Create a CV that is tailored to the placement you are applying for when submitting your application. Make sure to highlight the specific skills you have that are relevant to the job you are applying for, so that the employer can see that you have the required skills and always research the company before applying to show that you are interested."

*– Kennis Tang, Media Production student*

"Don't apply to just one placement and hope that you get it. Find a couple of placements that you like the sound of and apply to all of them. It's better to turn someone down than to get rejected without a back-up. Don't take rejection personally. If you do get rejected, don't get disheartened, instead flip it into a positive experience and ask for feedback on your application to see where you could improve next time."

*– Emily May Drummond, Media Production student*

---

## Hear from the Experts

"When you're applying for placements, never send the same application to multiple employers. Always personalise each approach in some way. I've received numerous applications over the years where it's obvious that this has been done, and in each case I've never considered them. As the employer, you want to feel like the applicant has taken the time to write an application specific to your role. This will make you more likely to stand out. One time, an applicant for one of our placements didn't even change the company name in the cover letter! That is a really basic mistake that can be easily avoided with due care and attention."

*– Tom Walters, Account Director, The Dairy*

"Searching for a job can feel like a tiresome and never-ending task. When you have to complete long application forms that never seem to amount to anything, it can make you feel deflated. Having the resilience to continue the search is so important. If I didn't get through to the next stage in a job application process, I would always feel a strange sense of positivity rather than dwell on rejection. I learnt more about what I really wanted, and it meant I was closer to finding the job that was the right fit for me and aligned with my values. The right job will come up, it always does, even if it's just a steppingstone on your career journey."

*– Millie Hegarty, business owner and entrepreneur*

"So, on the off chance there was a job, I sent them my portfolio and said in the meantime 'hey, I really love the work. I love the research and the rationale that you create. Can we just have a chat?'. There's so much value in just saying 'I love your agency's work. Can we just have a conversation?' Which we did. We had a conversation, and they still weren't hiring."

*– Shauna Wilkinson, Creative, Ginger Root*

"Put yourself out there, employers are not going to be calling out for you. Unless you put yourself there, they're not going to find you. You really have to promote yourself. You have to email. The worst thing that someone can do by emailing someone is that they can say No – that's the worst thing that's going to happen to you. You're not going to die. It's all fine. Send the email or go to the event or speak to that person. It can be really intimidating, but you've got to put yourself out there."

*– Rebecca Lewis, Senior Creative Content Editor, Getty Images*

---

# Interviewing for Your Placement

If your application is successful, you will hopefully be invited to interview for the role. There are many ways in which you might be interviewed: it may be one-to-one, by a panel, a group interview, through an assessment centre (where you take part in psychometric and other sorts of tests), by telephone, a video interview, or by a technical, formal or informal test, for example. The most likely form of interview for a placement is face-to-face, by telephone or via video call. Although interviews can be daunting, just remember that the people interviewing are rooting for you. They want you to do your best, but they are also looking for the best person to fit the role, and importantly someone they will want to work with.

---

### Hear from the Expert

"When you do have an interview, it's more about whether or not you're going to fit into the work culture of where you're applying. So if you're doing a sales job, they want to know that you're going to work hard, but they also want to know that you're going to be a laugh and that they can sit next to you 9–5 everyday, and you're not going to be a bore or a miserable person. Just try and let your personality shine through and it should be fine."

*– Kyle Lord, Digital Technologist*

---

The interview will often include competency-based questions that each candidate will answer. These questions usually ask you to give an example of a competency you implemented, and it is a good idea to prepare for answering these interview questions in a structured manner. The BECTU *Creative Toolkit* (creativetoolkit.org.uk) and *BBC Careers* (careers.bbc.co.uk/) both have useful advice about preparing for interviews using the STAR mnemonic:

*   S – Situation: give an example of a situation where you used a competency or behaviour
*   T – Task/target: What were you trying to achieve? What were your responsibilities and objectives?
*   A – Action: detail what action you took and why
*   R – Result: describe the results you achieved and what conclusions you were able to make

An additional R can be added to the mnemonic:

*   R – Reflection: consider what you learned from the situation and how you might use this to inform future actions

## Exercise: Answering Competency-based Questions Using the STAR(R) Technique

This exercise gives you an opportunity to practise answering examples of competency-based questions using the **STAR(R) technique**. It will enable you to find answers that are targeted to the role that you will be interviewed for by basing your answers on your performance in a practical group media project while on your course. Complete the table below and remember to think of specific examples to illustrate your points. It is a good idea to say how much experience you have already and how much you wish to develop further.

| Question | Answer | | | | |
| --- | --- | --- | --- | --- | --- |
| Question | Situation | Task | Action | Result | Reflection |
| Give an example of when you worked effectively in a team | | | | | |
| Question | Situation | Task | Action | Result | Reflection |
| Give an example of your problem-solving | | | | | |
| Question | Situation | Task | Action | Result | Reflection |
| Talk about a time when you used your own initiative | | | | | |

Now add to the table by creating your own examples of the types of questions that could relate to the placements that you plan to apply for. Use the STAR(R) technique to prepare your answers.

Once you have drafted your responses on paper, ask a peer or friend to ask you the questions, so you can practise answering them out loud using the structured STAR(R) technique.

Keep practising this technique until it becomes second nature to you. In an interview situation you may need a couple of seconds to think of a relevant situation, but by following the STAR(R) technique your answers will sound confident, composed and clear.

# Mock Interviews

Following on from practising answering interview questions on your own and with a friend, it is a good idea to take advantage of the opportunity to practise your interview technique in a **mock interview**. Your university's careers department may offer a mock interviewing service. There are also apps available online where you can take part in an interview simulation.

---

**Hear from the Expert**

"I took courses for mock interviews, which I find very useful because you learn that you don't need to sound like a robot or to present this fake version of yourself that you think employers might want. Just be yourself. Because in the beginning, if we're being honest, you're not really going to get hired based on your experience because you might have little to none. So it's just about the energy that you're bringing to the workplace and your personality."

*– Alexa Garcia Degante, Account Executive, Framework Design*

---

# Face-to-face interviews

If your interview is taking place face to face, there are a number of things you may want to consider. Make sure you arrive at the location early – for example, by catching an earlier train than you need to. You don't want to miss your interview, and the interviewer certainly doesn't want it to start by hearing why you are late.

---

**Student Voice**

"Make sure that you're on time to everything. There's nothing worse than being late for an interview. It just shows that you're not interested, that you don't really care too much. If there's an emergency, just let the employer know and apologise."

*– Zachary Omitowoju, Media Production Graduate*

---

**Hear from the Expert**

"I'm currently interviewing half a dozen students for placements and I've noticed that all of them have turned up to the interview between three and five minutes early. It's important because if you're there three minutes early, I know that you're going to be there early for my clients and not keep them waiting."

*– Simon Elliott, Managing Director, Diversity Agency*

---

You may be wondering how you need to dress. The best answer is to do some research prior to the interview. Find out what style of dress the employees wear by looking for evidence in promotional material or images online. If the placement provider has visited your university to do a talk, what did they wear? Thinking about these things will give you an idea of how you should present yourself for the interview.

## Student Voice

"In terms of preparation, my first tip is if you want the part then dress the part. Whether you're in person or on camera, look presentable during the interview."

– *Zachary Omitowoju, Media Production graduate*

Show your friendliness and enthusiasm through positive body language and facial expressions. This should happen as soon as you enter the building, but is especially important as you enter the interview room. Smile as you enter, make good eye contact and pay attention to your body posture. The interviewing panel will smile back, and it will create a positive atmosphere.

## Student Voice

"I'd highly recommend always doing your best to make eye contact. It shows that you're interested in the interviewer and that you're paying attention, which is something that I quickly had to remember. Take a note of any feedback that your interviewer gives you."

– *Zachary Omitowoju, Media Production graduate*

If you are asked if you want a drink, it is probably best to stick to water. There will probably be water to hand, and it may help to take a couple of sips if your mouth becomes dry during the interview.

As you are asked questions, you can demonstrate your attentiveness through active listening. Again, this will include maintaining eye contact, but you can also nod to show you are listening, and even repeat back part of the question. You can do the latter as you think briefly about your answer. For example:

Interviewer:   Tell us about a time when you used your own initiative.
You:            A time when I used my own initiative?…or
You:            I used my own initiative recently when I…

Finally, the interviewer will probably ask if you have any questions. It is a good idea to have a couple of questions up your sleeve, especially if it helps to show that you are genuinely interested in the job or the organisation.

Once your interview is over, leave in the same positive way that you entered.

## Hear from the Experts

"I like it when our candidates have got questions for us, and I like it when people have done research on our organisation. Even if it's just briefly looking at the website. I think that shows a bit of respect for what we are offering as an opportunity."

– *Megan Shore, Programmes Manager, Ignite!*

"You need to leave a memorable moment for people when you're interviewing with them. So be yourself. If you're a little bit mental and you swear a lot, do those things because if they don't hire you, that just means you're not the fit for that company. Someone else will accept you on that basis. So just be yourself and try and leave them with something that when they look back to all the different candidates, they go, you know that one person, they were interesting. I want to bring them in again and you'll find that it works. This industry is incredible. I don't think I could have succeeded in any other industry because we're all just a little bit weird and wonderful."

*– Stephan Hayward, Managing Director, Framework Design*

"In our line of work, we have a lot of clients and deal with many stakeholders, so being well organised is really, really, important. We like someone who can evidence that, whether it is working on a university project where they lead something, or they can plan with a Gantt chart. Those things are music to our ears because we know that person isn't going to forget about something that we need to do because it will be on a plan, and they'll be able to communicate well with other people."

*– Simon Elliott, Managing Director, Diversity Agency*

# Remote Interviews

## Hear from the Expert

"In a Zoom interview – it goes without saying – make sure your camera and microphone work. Don't fidget and make sure you look at your webcam, rather than around the room."

*– Kyle Lord, Digital Technologist*

Interviewing via video has become more common place in recent times and *BBC Careers* (careers.bbc.co.uk/) have some useful tips for preparing for remote interviews:

* block out distractions – don't be overly casual, be heard, don't be interrupted, be in a place where you can answer the questions to your best ability
* technical preparation – make sure your sound and microphone are on, that the device is in a secure position and at an angle where you can be seen clearly
* be authentic – let your true personality shine. Make eye contact, avoid watching yourself on the screen and look directly into the camera

(adapted from bbc.co.uk/careers/how-to-apply/interview-tips)

It goes without saying that it is very important that your camera is switched on and working. This will probably be the first time your potential placement provider will get to see you, so the first impression is very important. Make sure you are dressed appropriately, that you are perfectly in frame in a tidy neutral setting or with a blurred background. Ensure that you are not going to be interrupted by flatmates, family members or pets.

# Panel Interviews

A panel interview is a situation where you are interviewed by a number of people who are in a variety of positions from the employing organisation. Members of the panel will take turns to ask questions, so you need to be prepared to interact with everyone present.

In a panel interview 'you must make an effort to make regular eye contact with all panel members in reasonably equal measure. You must build rapport with each and every one of them. Easier said than done, but eye contact is an excellent start' (Innes, 2016: 51).

When answering a question at a panel interview, first, 'focus on the panel member who asked you the question but, as you make your points, steer your gaze steadily from one panel member to another' and avoid 'focusing too much of your attention on just one panel member' (Innes, 2016: 51).

If you have never experienced a panel interview before, it may be worth getting together with a group of your peers to role-play some panel interview scenarios. You can take advice from your university careers department too.

# Group Interviews

An employer may wish to conduct a group interview, rather than an interview set-up that is conducted by a panel but interviews candidates for the job separately. In group interviews, candidates are assessed simultaneously for problem-solving and teamwork when completing group tasks.

As Innes (2016: 76) points out, one of the motivations for an employer holding a group interview is 'to identify how you work within a team [and] what role you naturally fulfil'. You can put your experience from your university team projects to good use here by demonstrating that you can work well in a team, as Innes suggests:

> Working well within a group means listening, cooperating, communicating, generating ideas and solutions. [In a group interview, do] you help the group to achieve its objectives or are you more of a hindrance? (Innes, 2016: 76)

Just as we suggested earlier when offering advice about interviews in general, you need to be calm and confident about your own teamwork abilities, and you can only do this by being yourself. The employer will be looking for a candidate whom they will enjoy working with every day, and this is just as important as letting them know that you can do the job.

─┤ **Hear from the Experts** ├──────────────────────────

"We spend a lot of time together in the office. Having a good team fit, being approachable, is what we look for – being a person that we can see will gel within the team."

*– Simon Elliott, Managing Director, Diversity Agency*

"I think most people know that you're early on in your career, so you might not have had lots of experience yet. But as long as you show real enthusiasm for learning and taking on the opportunity, I think that's what makes me feel confident about working with somebody."

*– Megan Shore, Programmes Manager*

"It doesn't have to be perfect you know. In life we strive to make something perfect and never actually create anything. Something is better than nothing. Obviously put a bit of effort in and so it's not a really poor effort. It's interesting to see someone's passion. That is the start point, what excites them. I'm very lucky to have a really talented team around me that can make our business look good, which is fantastic, but that's because they have various passions. I've got someone who's hugely passionate about development and code base. And then I've got someone else in the team who is really passionate about typography. Those two people don't always get each other's passion points, but the combination is superb. So just understanding what makes someone tick. And what's in the portfolio. And as I say often, the fear is that people think, 'oh, it's not going to be good enough or it's not perfected enough' but it's just an idea. It also shows an employer that you are making a bit of an effort and shows where you are passionate."

*– Simon Elliott, Managing Director, Diversity Agency*

──────────────────────────────────────

# Applying for Freelance/Self-employed Positions

So far in this chapter we have given you advice and support on applying for and being interviewed for placements that have been advertised. We have also offered guidance on making speculative applications. We have also discussed how you can generate your own project. We are now going to guide you in pitching for this type of placement. Being able to pitch is an important skill, particularly for people working for themselves.

An **elevator pitch** is a way to sell yourself, an idea or a service. In the context of finding a work experience placement, it is about selling yourself to a potential placement employer. An elevator pitch has the following requirements:

- it should be 90 seconds long (you can plan your timings on the basis of three words per second, so your 90-second pitch will be approximately 270 words)
- it should have a clear goal – what do you want to achieve from doing it? For example, to sell yourself to a placement provider
- it should help to solve a problem – in this context, it solves the problem of the employer finding someone to work for them

- it should be concise – keep it simple and to the point
- it should be aware of its audience – you need to address them in a way that grabs their attention

## Exercise: Preparing an Elevator Pitch

You need to prepare an elevator pitch in advance of approaching employers for freelance positions. Complete the form below to plan and prepare for your elevator pitch. Rehearse your pitch, maybe in front of a mirror to check body language and fluency, and to avoid reading from a script.

**Elevator Pitch Planner**

| Content | Your notes | Timing (3 words per second) |
| --- | --- | --- |
| Your name | | |
| Welcome and introduction (establish what you want to achieve through the pitch) | | |
| Describe your area of expertise that is appropriate to the employer | | |
| Talk about the skills and experience you have to offer | | |
| Highlight your unique selling point (USP) | | |
| Identify why you are needed to the employer | | |
| Close on a call-to-action that suggests what should happen now | | |

# Applications, Interviews and Your Wellbeing

There is no denying that applying for a placement can be very stressful. You may feel an overwhelming pressure to succeed and that everything hangs on making the right decision. However, it is important to remember that any placement you undertake is simply an *experience* of work – a chance to try things out and see how it feels for you. Your over-anxious need to succeed may be driven by perfectionism. As Mair (2019: 86–87) argues:

> Perfectionism is based on fear; fear that you're not good enough; that you have to prove yourself constantly and that nothing less than the absolute best is acceptable; that if you don't achieve the highest results, your life will be a disaster.

At this stage in your education and life you have the opportunity to test whether a job is suitable for you – not whether you are suitable for the job. Focus on being comfortable in yourself and applying for a job that you feel has integrity and fits with your mindset. This will be more important than the fear of making a mistake. Apply the same approach when preparing for your interview.

Below is a checklist of things you can do to make the application and interview process for a placement a less daunting and more positive experience:

- Have a positive mindset – your employer will most likely have been in the same position that you are in when they were your age, so they will understand your position and will be rooting for you. The placement may convince you that this is the type of job you want to go into when you graduate. If not, at least you have got some experience under your belt that you can add to your CV and learn from
- Form groups to search together – make the search for placements less stressful by turning it into a group activity. Team up with your peers to look for opportunities. Remember that you are not alone, and you can always discuss the process of your search with your friends or tutor. You can also see your university careers advisors for help and support
- Don't compare yourself to others – your personal goals and principals won't be the same as everybody else's. You are an individual. Look for a placement that suits *you*
- Cope with rejection – finding a placement might take several attempts. You may have to practise the application process and redraft your CV/cover email numerous times. You may have to go through the interview process several times in order to improve your technique. Remember that it is a learning process. The beauty about doing this as a student is that it helps you to build your resilience in readiness for when you graduate
- Create goals beyond the application and interview – don't dwell on the application and interview as an end point. See it in perspective. What are you going to do after you have had the interview? Take some time out? See some friends? Go to the cinema? Buy a treat for yourself? Creating a goal beyond the application and interview helps to give you something to look forward to

Finally, look after yourself. Learn to relax and 'switch off'.

## Hear from the Experts

"I'm a big advocate for wellbeing and mental health. Exercise, move your body. Get the endorphins going, eat well and do what's best for you. Don't focus on what other people are doing. Take breaks from social media. I can't stress that enough. Read a book. Do something that's good for *your soul* and makes you feel like you're glowing from the inside out! Just take care of yourself, take a step back. Find something that makes you completely detach and relax. It's just so important. I can't stress that enough."

*– Laura Savage, Marketing Director, DeCantillon Films*

"The key thing, I think, is not to stress about it. I didn't go straight into the industry and that was the best decision for me. I didn't entirely know which way I wanted to go. Don't get into a stress about it because there's no need. It's about being confident in your own skills, in your own abilities, being confident in what you have to bring to the table. That you are good at what they're looking for now and that you have the necessary skills. And tell people. Make your case. Tell them why they should hire you. Make sure that you build that confidence because, again, that will push you right up there. When you're confident and reliable, you're going to get work. People want somebody who is confident in themselves: they want somebody that knows what they're doing."

*– Laura Savage, Marketing Director, DeCantillon Films*

# Conclusion

In this chapter we have given you some help and advice on searching for and applying for placements, and for creating your own placement opportunity and negotiating a brief. We have provided some practical information on organising and keeping on top of your placement application process, and for preparing and practising for interviews. We have also included some tips and hints to support your wellbeing while you secure a placement. By now you should feel excited and enthused.

Once your placement has been secured, the next chapter will help you to get the best out of your experience.

## Further Reading

BBC (n.d.) *BBC Careers* [website]. Available at: https://careers.bbc.co.uk/. This website provides a useful guide to how the BBC use competency-based interviews.

Innes, James (2016) *The Interview Book: How to Prepare and Perform at Your Best in Any Interview*. Harlow: Pearson Education. This book provides a comprehensive overview of how to plan, prepare and perform in interviews.

Mair, David (2019) *The Student Guide to Mindfulness*. London: Sage. This book is an accessible guide to how mindfulness can help students.

Williams, Lynn (2021) *Ultimate Interview: 100s of Sample Questions and Answers for Interview Success*. London: Kogan Page. This book provides you with practical advice for preparing for interviews, including examples of interview questions and answers.

# 10

# PREPARING FOR YOUR WORK EXPERIENCE

## Making the Transition from Student to Professional

## Introduction

In the previous few chapters of this book, we helped to prepare you for finding, applying for, and being interviewed for a work experience placement. In the remaining chapters we are going to help you to get the best out of your work experience, to learn to reflect on it, and to use it to enhance your employability. In this chapter we will begin by helping you to make the transition from being a student to becoming a professional, maximising the success of any work experience you undertake. The chapter will also give you some practical pointers to help you to track your progress, and that will be useful for reflecting on your experience after the placement.

The aims and outcomes of this chapter are:

- to carry out further research into the placement provider's organisation in readiness for your work experience
- to consider your professional identity during your time on the placement
- to keep a daily record of your work that will aid your reflection on the experience
- to build your professional network
- to look after your health and wellbeing during the placement

List of exercises in this chapter:

- Researching the sector
- Researching your work experience organisation
- Modelling your professional identity

# Planning for Your Placement

Once you have secured your placement you should start to make plans for it. You will benefit from finding out as much as you can about your employer. This will be very useful research for when you go on placement, regardless of what type of placement you do, whether it is on location with a freelance director or in an office for a large corporate organisation.

## Sector Awareness

Employers in the media and creative sector look for employees who show evidence that they have an awareness and understanding of the sector they are wanting to go into. Sometimes referred to as having commercial awareness, this is an understanding of the business, its aims and how you might help those aims to be achieved. It is about showing that you understand what makes the organisation successful, and how the organisation makes money or survives. This also refers to having knowledge of the industry and sector that you are interested in.

Before and during your work experience you are advised to deepen your understanding of the organisation and the sector, and work on strategies for evidencing that you have this awareness. Having commercial awareness is an employability skill that can be developed and improved. It is important because it can assist you in helping your employer achieve their aims and to add value to the organisation.

## Exercise: Researching the Sector

Once you have a good idea of the organisation you will be working in for your work experience, you will benefit from researching about the sector more broadly. This will take you a step further to developing your commercial awareness.

You can find relevant information by looking at the trade press or sector magazines. There may be industry reports you can consult. You can also explore the network organisations and professional associations that exist within the sector (see Chapter 2 where we listed some of these sources). You should be able to find a lot of information from professional social media too. Conduct some research into the sector using the areas listed below as a guide:

- the sorts of jobs available in the sector
- the way most people are employed – full-time, part-time, freelance, temporary contracts
- the pay structures and promotion prospects
- what skills are required for working in the sector
- if there are skills gaps in the sector and where these are
- in which areas employment opportunities are growing, and which are declining
- the current health of the sector

- the current trends and developments in the sector
- how the sector is represented in the press and media
- case studies and interviews with people working in the sector

Now that you have surveyed the sector you are working in, you should prepare for your placement by doing some research on your work experience organisation. The next exercise will help you.

## Exercise: Researching Your Work Experience Organisation

Before you start your work experience, and when you are undertaking it, you can develop your commercial awareness further by answering the questions below about the organisation. Answers to many of these questions can be found on the organisation's website and through industry publications and the trade press. You should also check out the organisation's social media profile, and search for any mention of them in the media. You can also refer to the career case study exercise undertaken in Chapter 4, where you conducted research into a career area or job of interest to you.

Ask the following questions of the organisation you are working in:

- What does the organisation do?
- What product or service is the organisation concerned with?
- What is the organisation's mission and what are its aims?
- Does the organisation have commercial priorities? If so, what are they?
- How many employees are there in the organisation?
- Who owns and controls the organisation?
- Who are their clients/customers? Can you find any 'customer' testimonials that will give you an idea of the organisation's relationship with its clients?
- What market are they in and what share of the market do they occupy?
- Who are their competitors and how do they relate to each other?
- Who are the key people in the organisation?
- How is the organisation managed? What does their organisational chart (or hierarchy) look like?
- Are there any political or economic issues that might affect the organisation?
- What are the corporate social responsibility (CSR) and equality, diversity and inclusion (EDI) policies of the organisation? Are there any other such policies to note?
- What do you understand of the job role you are undertaking for your work experience?
- What are the duties and responsibilities of your role and those of your colleagues?
- What is the work culture of the organisation?

You are advised to keep a record of the answers you locate. In Chapter 12 we will encourage you to produce a reflective report about your work experience, so your notes will also help with that.

While on your work experience, you can take opportunities to demonstrate the commercial awareness you have developed through the research exercises above. Be confident in the knowledge you have gathered about the sector and organisation, but also try to show that you want to learn more.

# Making the Transition From Student to Professional

We are now going to consider the development of your professional identity and making the transition from being a student to becoming a professional in the workplace. This will help you to get the very best out of your work experience. In Chapter 3 we looked at the skills and qualities that employers look for in graduate employees. It is worth revisiting Chapter 3 now and thinking about what professional qualities you could enhance or develop.

## Exercise: Modelling Your Professional Identity

Below is a list of the types of professional qualities that are important to develop and demonstrate while you are on a placement. As you read the list, think about how you might model your own professionalism in the specific context of the placement organisation you will be working in.

From the list below choose some of the professional qualities that you would like to focus on during your placement. Think about how you will approach, demonstrate and improve each of the qualities you have selected. You can also think about how each of these qualities might manifest as unprofessional behaviour.

Professional qualities:

- appearing interested, motivated and enthusiastic
- showing initiative
- having a positive attitude
- working effectively to a brief and meeting any deadlines given
- learning from mistakes
- being reflective
- receiving feedback constructively
- showing a collegiate approach and demonstrating empathy
- being a team player
- demonstrating a potential for leadership
- paying attention to written communication, such as spelling and grammar
- having good presentation skills
- being aware of email etiquette and using appropriate formality
- showing cultural awareness and tolerance
- making appropriate use of social media both in and out of the workplace

- practising good verbal communication skills
- seeing a project through to the end
- working independently where appropriate
- being punctual and attending well
- being well organised
- showing a willingness to take on new challenges
- demonstrating discretion, tact and respecting confidentiality
- showing confidence

# Networking

**Networking** is an important aspect of career development that is worth paying attention to while you are on a placement or engaged with work experience. Consider what long-term benefits you need to get out of the work experience. For example, are you looking to make potential contacts for the future, including colleagues within the organisation and connections within the wider sector? The latter might include the clients that the organisation works with, the professional associations they belong to and other professional networks they are part of.

The benefits of networking are:

- creating potential access for future jobs
- finding support with career development through mentoring
- finding information about developments within the sector
- building connections with like-minded people to learn from and share ideas with
- being noticed and making yourself available for potential jobs

You can approach networking while on your placement in one or more of the ways outlined below.

You can network through face-to-face contact with colleagues while on your placement. Apart from informally interacting with them on a daily basis, you can try speaking up in meetings and attending networking events and social gatherings after work. If you have the opportunity, make every effort to attend any relevant conferences, festivals and trade shows.

Consider getting involved with some career coaching, if the organisation you have been placed with employs a mentor. Mentoring services may also be available through your university's careers department.

## Hear from the Experts

"Make sure you network professionally – whether that's face to face or through LinkedIn. You will naturally make new connections during placements just by working alongside people, but make sure you add these people on LinkedIn and stay connected beyond the placement. In the long term, you want to remain at the front of people's minds. You never know where those connections could lead you in the future."

*– Tom Walters, Account Director, The Dairy*

"Networking is important. If you use LinkedIn, there is always an event [that] pops up in my page and my feeds, like a freelance event or there is a media statement. Also, people don't realise that you are surrounded with the people who already work in the industry that can help if you just directly ask them."

*– Eugene Kogut, Videographer*

"If I went to a networking event, I'd often approach the editor/presenter and tell them a bit about the experience I'd got so far and ask if I could shadow or get some work experience. Often, they'd say yes and tell me to drop them an email. They've been in your shoes once, so will often want to help if they can! If I didn't hear back in two weeks' time, I'd send a follow-up email because it's so easy for your email to get lost – they're busy people!"

*– Emma Snow, Journalist, BBC*

"The freelancers that are out there could give you advice as well on how to get into the industry. A lot of freelancers worked for production companies first and gained all that experience and networks before then turning to the freelance world. So network, it's very much who you know as well as what you know. And with networking in mind, I always use LinkedIn and email. I will contact people that we want to do business with through emails. And make them a personal read. Make sure you've done your research and you know the company. Maybe research a few projects that they've worked on. Just start to build your network of people and contacts so you're not doing it cold when it comes to graduation."

*– Ben Newth, Head of Video at a corporate video company*

---

Get involved in the relevant online interest groups in the jobs sector on your preferred professional social media accounts. Below are some professional and trade associations that represent their members in specific industry areas. Note that some of these associations might require you to sign up and pay for membership, which is not recommended while you are a student (unless they offer student discounts). Consider following the relevant ones on your professional social media accounts and take part in online discussions.

- British Interactive Media Association (BIMA) (bima.co.uk) – a professional association for those working in interactive media
- Chartered Institute of Marketing (CIM) (cim.co.uk) – a professional association for those working in marketing
- Chartered Institute of Public Relations (CIPR) (cipr.co.uk) – a professional association for those working in public relations

- Institute of British Advertisers (ISBA) (isba.org.uk) – a professional association for those working in advertising
- Producers Alliance for Cinema and Television (PACT) (pact.co.uk) – an organisation for independent film and television producers
- International Moving Image Society (IMIS) (societyinmotion.com) – an international community for the moving image industry
- The Association for UK Interactive Entertainment (ukie) (ukie.org.uk) – the trade body for the games and interactive entertainment industry

Also research any support networks that exist in your sector that are relevant to you. Most sectors have support networks that offer support and guidance to people working within the sector. Many of these are aimed at supporting a diverse range of people and helping them to access the industry. There are some examples below, but you may wish to search for others that are relevant to your own career interest area and social and cultural background. You can use search terms such as 'support networks for the ... industry', inserting the sector you are interested in. You can also look at their LinkedIn, Facebook, Instagram and Twitter/X pages.

- ACCESSVFX (accessvfx.org) – an organisation pursuing diversity and inclusion in the visual FX, animation and games industries
- Creative Access (creativeaccess.org.uk) – a networking organisation for communities that are under-represented in the creative industries
- The Creative Industries Federation (stage.creativeindustriesfederation.com) – a networking and campaigning organisation for the creative industries
- Creative Pool (creativepool.com) – a networking organisation for the creative sector
- Deaf & Disabled People in TV (ddptv.org) – a networking organisation for deaf, disabled and neuro-divergent professionals working in TV
- Film + TV Charity (filmtvcharity.org.uk) – an organisation providing support for people working in film and television
- The Guild of Television Camera Professionals (gtc.org.uk) – a member organisation for professionals working in all areas of production
- Mama Youth Project (mamayouth.org.uk) – a support organisation for young people from diverse communities wanting to enter the media industry
- Mediatrust (mediatrust.org) – a charity working with media and community groups
- Production Base (productionbase.co.uk) – a networking organisation for freelancers
- The Production Guild of Great Britain (productionguild.com) – a support/ membership organisation for film and TV drama professionals
- Publishers Association (publishers.org.uk) – a membership organisation for the publishing industry
- The Radio Academy (radioacademy.org) – a networking organisation for people working in radio

- Soulsound (soulsound.co.uk) – a membership organisation for supporting sound engineers
- The TV Collective (thetvcollective.org) – a group supporting filmmakers from diverse backgrounds
- Women in Film and Television Network (WFTVN) (wftvn.org.uk) – a membership organisation supporting women in the media and creative sector

As you come across these industry contacts and organisations during your placement/s, you are advised to collate all of this information into a database to build up your network, and keep it regularly updated.

## Health and Wellbeing

Many networking and support organisations offer health and wellbeing support to their members. For example, a search for networking organisations in the film and television industry will list organisations such as Film + TV Charity (filmtvcharity. org.uk), which offers 24/7 mental health support for people in their industry. It is a good idea to seek out similar appropriate support for yourself in preparation for your placement or work experience. Your university will have support mechanisms in place that you can access, but there are also ways you can look out for your own health and wellbeing while on placement. You can use the following self-help tips and hints to assist you:

- Try to find a balance between work and leisure, making time for activities you find relaxing and taking good care of your physical health. The SHED acronym is helpful – sleep, hydration, exercise and diet
- Breathe slowly. Breathe in for the count of four... and breathe out for the count of four
- It is helpful to write down your feelings, even if it's a note on your mobile. This technique helps you to make sense of what you're feeling. You can make this a regular habit, doing it at the beginning or end of the day

(adapted from filmtvcharity.org.uk/your-support/mental-wellbeing/
freelancer-wellbeing-hub/freelancer-support-resources/)

Another idea is to set yourself a positive goal after the first day of your work experience or at the end of the week. This can be anything you find relaxing, such as meeting or phoning a friend, treating yourself to a nice healthy meal when you get home, going for a walk, or doing other physical activities. You might find it helpful to engage in some mindfulness and meditation too. You can also improve your own wellbeing by helping others. You can form a small support group with your peers and regularly get in touch with each other throughout your placements to provide mutual help, encouragement and advice. Supporting others like this can be very rewarding and help to improve your own sense of worth.

---

( **Hear from the Expert** )

"In my workday I make sure that I go on a half an hour walk and listen to a mindset podcast. The fresh air is so good for my mental health and making me feel relaxed. The exercise is also important when I'm sitting down for most of the day. I make sure to drink enough water and eat a healthy lunch to increase productivity. I also make sure that I have a safe space to go if I ever feel overwhelmed and a person who I can confide in if necessary."

*– Millie Hegarty, business owner and entrepreneur*

---

# Advice on Making Plans for Your Professional Behaviour While on Your Placement

There are a number of things you can do to help yourself to get the most out of any work experience while you are undertaking it. Take advantage of as much advice as you can gather, including tips and hints for success on your placement. The TV Watercooler website (tvwatercooler.org/) has a very useful guide on being a runner that offers detailed tips and hints on how to make the best of the opportunity (tvwatercooler.org/latest/tips-for-tv-runners). These are useful for any student or someone in the early stages of a career (not just runners). Here is just a small selection of the advice they offer:

1    When you are asked to do a boring job ... do not pull a face and say, 'You must really hate me' ... no matter how menial the task, approach [it] with enthusiasm and perform to the best of your abilities

2    Your team will sometimes talk a lot of shorthand and use industry language. Don't pretend to know what something is or means if you don't know. No one expects you to know everything. Ask someone to explain it to you at an appropriate moment and don't be embarrassed – it shows you were taking it all in and you are keen to learn

3    Get into the habit of writing a 'To Do' list every day and ticking off your tasks as you do them. At the end of the day, start writing tomorrow's list before you leave and copy across everything you didn't get done today. This will help you to focus on the varied tasks you have been given by the entire team and get you used to prioritising

4    Don't be afraid to offer/input ideas. Learn when to sit in the corner and keep quiet and pick your moment carefully to offer your input. Whether it is well received or not will be determined largely by your timing

5    You will earn extra brownie points if you check if anyone needs anything doing before you prepare to leave

6    If you are due to finish at 18:00, prepare yourself to stay until 18:30 or later. Don't arrange to meet your mate down the pub at 18:10. Sometimes work can overflow and to go beyond the call of duty without angst will be expected. Just don't be rushing for the door on the dot

(The TV Watercooler, n.d.)

Don't be afraid to ask others for tips and hints like these before embarking on your work experience. You can ask students who have already been on a placement to give you advice, or ask your tutor or your university careers advisor. After you have had experience of a placement, you can pass advice onto your peers.

# Preparing for Documenting and Reflecting on Your Placement

In Chapter 12 we will give you guidance on producing a report on your work experience. The following advice will help you to gather evidence now to reflect upon at a later date.

- Keep a work log – while on placement you are advised to keep a log of what you have done each day as you go along. This is a descriptive set of notes of what you did hour-by-hour. It will be useful for when you reflect on and analyse your work experience when producing a placement report.
- Gather evidence for your report/reflective work – while on placement gather evidence that you can use in your report. This can be screen shots and links to the organisation's website, company reports and any work you produced while on placement (for example, a press release, a blog post, an article, or link to a video). Be aware of copyright and confidentiality issues. Make sure you check with and obtain permission from the employer for any material you use.
- Document the experience – for your reflective report you can document the experience with photos and video clips. Again, make sure you get permission first. You can take photos/videos that reflect the work culture of the organisation (for example, the work environment, your workspace, colleagues, social aspects of work, photos that reflect the work culture). Of course, how you do this will look very different if you are in a remote working environment, but it will be interesting and useful for your experience and for your report if you can find a way to document your placement experience.
- Keep a diary – a diary can form a more personal record of the placement experience. For example, you can record how you feel and how you respond to situations, to any issues that have arisen, and to things you have learned on the job. It is a good idea to get into the habit of making an entry at the end of every working day.

## Hear from the Experts

"Building rapport is a priority to have a happy workplace as well as gaining a network and using it to your best abilities. Communication, talking and giving and receiving clear instructions and doing your job to the best of your ability."

– Ed Corteen, Content Producer, The Coaching Manual

"Communication is key. I was freelancing so it was really important that I scheduled in regular phone calls, so that I was in the loop. Be enthusiastic, even if it's something that you're not that necessarily into or know what you're doing – just throw yourself into it, be enthusiastic and it will pay off."

*– Noushka Seher, International Account Manager*

# Planning for Remote Working

It may be the case that you will undertake **remote working** during your placement. As we pointed out previously in the book, this is quite commonplace in the media and creative industries. If you are working from home, you will need to plan your work–life balance so that you make a distinction between work time and personal time. You may also want to separate your place of work from your place of relaxation (even if you are having to work in a small student apartment).

• Set up a work area – this could even be the desk in your room. If possible, place your workstation by a window so you get some natural light and can look outside occasionally
• Avoid distractions – tell housemates that you are working and to please keep the noise down where possible. Put your phone away or turn it off for a while. You can look at it during your lunchbreak to catch up with friends
• Stick to working day hours – even if the work is flexible, it will help to stick to a routine. Get up early before you start working so that you can have some 'me time' and breakfast before work
• Take some breaks – when working at home it is sometimes easy to get carried away with a task and sit staring at a computer screen for hours on end. It is important to have breaks away from the screen. Go and make a drink, make sure you have lunch. It may be a good idea to go outside and stretch your legs during your lunch break by having a short walk
• Keep in touch with the placement provider – you will get more out of the experience if you make regular contact with the employer. Give them daily email updates on your progress. They will no doubt organise online meetings or phone calls to brief you on your duties, so make the most of these by preparing a set of questions to ask. (It is better to do this than send several emails during the day when they are busy doing other things)
• At the end of the day put away your work paraphernalia – tidy up your desk, put your stationary away, hide the laptop. It will be easier for you to relax if you do not have work things in view

─┤ **Hear from the Experts** ├────────────────────────────────

"The company that I work for now, like many companies, adjusted to this working from home way of working. I think most companies are going that way. So I'm lucky enough to be able to work from home typically about three to four days a week. Normally on the others I'm on a shoot or I go up to the office. It's a bit of a commute, but I think in a way it's a testament to how the company treats their employees and allowing them to work from home. Specifically editing is something that you can do from home and if anything, you actually get more work done than you would do if you went into the office."

*– Sam Reynolds, Video and Motion Producer, Adtrak*

"Just because you may be working from home or working remotely somewhere, you still need to give across that professional image that you would if you're going into an office. So if you're going to see a client or colleague in the office, make sure your appearance is reflective of the environment and the role that you have. You still need to do that whether you are remote. You don't want to see one of your colleagues laid back on their bed with their laptop and still in their pyjamas at 10:00 o'clock on morning. It doesn't send the right impression and impressions are really important. Making sure that you've got that professional appearance and that you approach everything in that professional manner is important when working remotely."

*– Simon Elliott, Managing Director, Diversity Agency*

# Conclusion

In this chapter we have considered how to prepare for your placement by making the transition from being a student to becoming a professional. You have performed an exercise to help enhance your professional qualities in preparation for the placement and you have been encouraged to start a diary to document your daily experiences when you go into the workplace.

In the following chapter we will advise you on how to get the best out of your work experience with some supportive tips and hints on how to work effectively while on your placement.

## Further Reading

Neugebauer, John, and Evans-Brian, Jane (2009) *Making the Most of Your Placement.* London: Sage. This book covers every step of the work placement process. It is primarily aimed at business and management students, but can also assist you in the placement process from planning to making the most of the experience to aid your future career.

The Film and TV Charity (n.d.) *The Film and TV Charity* [website]. www.filmtvcharity. org.uk/your-support/mental-wellbeing/freelancer-wellbeing-hub/freelancer-support-resources/. This website has a very useful section on wellbeing resources for people in the media and creative industries.

The TV Watercooler (n.d.) 'Tips for TV Runners'. *The TV Watercooler* [website]. https:// tvwatercooler.org/latest/tips-for-tv-runners. This is a useful and easy-to-follow guide for production runners that you can download from the TV Watercooler site. It covers aspects such as attitude, communication and work hierarchies.

# 11

# GETTING THE BEST OUT OF YOUR WORK EXPERIENCE

## Modelling Professional Behaviours in the Workplace

## Introduction

In the previous chapter, we gave you some supportive suggestions on what you might do to prepare for your work experience placement. In this chapter we will help you to get the best out of your work experience, how to conduct yourself at work on a daily basis, and how to model your professional behaviour in the workplace. We will provide you with some supportive tips and hints on how to work effectively while on your work experience.

We will be referring to Chapter 3 where we discovered what skills and qualities employers are looking for in potential employees. We will be elaborating on the following areas, providing ideas of how you might recognise, demonstrate, develop, test out, improve and reflect on the various professional behaviours:

- digital housekeeping
- working to a brief
- organisation and time management
- teamwork
- communication
- personal qualities
- supervision and training
- awareness of the sector

Workplace skills are distinct from the specific technical and practical skills required to do the job (such as editing). They are transferable, can be developed and improved, and are relevant to many roles and areas of the sector. The workplace skills we are referring to include personal skills, such as people skills, communication skills and leadership, for example. They also include a range of **functional skills** which will help you to be more effective in your job, such as organisation and time management.

There are online courses available to help you improve your knowledge and awareness in the personal and functional skills areas mentioned above. For example, LinkedIn Learning and the Bright Network. Your university careers service may also offer training in these areas.

While on your work experience, you are advised to observe and learn from your colleagues about how they approach their work. Also take the opportunity to practise and try out skills that are new to you.

The aims and outcomes of this chapter are:

- to analyse and reflect on the professional behaviours that you already have
- to provide some tips and hints on how to work effectively while on your placement
- to examine some of the techniques you can use to increase your efficiency and effectiveness in the workplace

List of exercises in this chapter:

- Undertaking a digital housekeeping audit
- Developing teamwork qualities in the workplace
- Observing colleagues' approach to communication and interpersonal skills
- Identifying evidence of creativity and innovation

## Digital Housekeeping

You already have experience of digital housekeeping on a daily basis at university. For example, your use of software such as Microsoft Office (Word and PowerPoint) and your use of cloud storage and sharing systems such as OneDrive, Google Drive and Share-Point. While you are involved in your work experience it is a good idea to consider how to transfer this good practice to the workplace. At the most basic level, it can be something as simple as ensuring that your digital files are well managed, by naming them so that they are easy to locate, by keeping files in folders and by backing them up regularly. You can start your placement by analysing what practical skills you already have in file management and if there are any ways you can improve them.

Your work experience provider may have their own protocols for sharing and storing files as part of their cyber-security policy. For example, they may use encrypted, password-protected file sharing, rather than sending files by email attachment. It is worth checking if they have any special regulations for file management and sharing as part of your induction for the placement.

## Exercise: Undertaking a Digital Housekeeping Audit

We have suggested above that you will benefit from researching various aspects of the placement organisation's use of digital resources. Use the checklist below to make an audit of what is used and whether you need training to use it effectively. You can follow up the audit by seeking training in its use in the workplace. Training may be supplied by your work experience provider, your university or through online training.

| Digital resources | What is used in the organisation? | Do you need training to use it? YES/NO | Where will you access the training you need? |
|---|---|---|---|
| Operating system used (e.g. Mac or PC) | | | |
| Conferencing software used (e.g. Teams, Zoom, Skype) | | | |
| Calendars used (e.g. Outlook, Google Calendar, iCal) | | | |
| Digital storage and file sharing (e.g. WeTransfer, Dropbox, Google Drive, OneDrive, iCloud) | | | |
| Media hardware used (e.g. types of cameras, desktop computers, tablets, laptops) | | | |
| Media software used (e.g. Adobe, Avid or other editing systems) | | | |

# Email Etiquette

When it comes to writing emails, it is a good idea to survey the culture of the organisation to determine what type of language to use when addressing other colleagues. You don't want to risk being too casual, and at the same time it may not be appropriate to be overly formal if this does not fit the culture of the workplace. Do your colleagues address each other with 'Dear' or do they use greetings such as 'Hello' or 'Hi' at the beginning of emails? It often depends on how well the sender and recipient know each other. However, they may start an email thread with a more formal 'Dear' and then continue with a less formal 'Hi' as the exchange continues beyond the first message. Closing greetings are worth analysing too. Do colleagues use 'Sincerely', 'Kind regards', or 'Best wishes', for instance?

Another important aspect of **email etiquette** you should consider is to whom to send messages. If you are composing a message to a group, but need to keep their email addresses or names private due to data protection, is it more appropriate to write their email addresses in the Bcc (blind carbon copy) address line? If you receive an email which has been sent to a group of people using Cc (carbon copy), consider whether it is important that you 'reply to all' or if you only need to reply directly to the sender.

As you survey the email etiquette of the organisation you might notice other features, such as email signatures that list:

- a person's role in the organisation
- their qualifications
- links to their professional social media accounts
- a list of their recent prizes or awards

Colleagues might also state their preferred pronouns or include a link to an application that demonstrates how their name should be pronounced. Take a moment to consider how you might want to update your email signature to include any of the features listed above. Could you add your professional social media accounts or an award that you have won for a film you have entered into a festival?

## Online Protocol

Your placement might involve remote working. If this is the case, there is another set of digital protocols to consider. During online meetings, gauge when it is appropriate to have your camera switched on or off, when you should mute or unmute your microphone, how to use the chat feature and how to capture the attention of the meeting's chair by raising your hand. If you need to show any work or documents on screen, it is important to know how to use the screen sharing facility as well. If you are required to share rough edits of video work or any other digital files, you should check how your placement provider would prefer you to do this, following their rules regarding their cyber-security protocols.

## Organisation and Time Management

You have already had a lot of opportunity to practise your organisation and **time management** skills while on your degree course. You can carry this experience over to the workplace and aim to develop these areas further while on your work experience. You are advised to find out what the organisation's approach to time management is before you start. For example, you can find out how they manage their workflows and how they expect employees to do it.

Much of the work in the media and creative industries is likely to be project based. It is worth spending some time honing your project management, decision-making and problem-solving skills. This also links to working to a brief and to deadlines. These are all skill areas that potential employers will be looking for in their employees.

You will benefit from undertaking some training in the basics of project management. This is a skill area that is in demand in many organisations. It is very important if you are working for yourself or freelancing. Basic awareness of project management skills will be helpful to you during your work experience.

A project is limited by time and has a predetermined result. The project runs through phases and is determined by a budget, quality control and working to a deadline. Project briefs are usually broken down into stages (that have to be met within a certain time-frame if the project is not to be held up). You will assess what the project is to achieve, organising the staged activities, maintaining an overview of the whole project, solving problems as you go along and reviewing the success of the project. For successful project management, you will need to use other workplace skills too, such as leadership, communication skills and problem-solving skills.

There are many tools that can be used to enable effective project management and it is worth becoming familiar with them. Different organisations will use different tools, so you will need to find out what the organisation you are working with tends to use. The list of examples below is by no means exhaustive:

- Microsoft Project – software that helps project managers in planning, organising resources, tracking progress and analysing workstreams
- Skype, Zoom, Teams – applications that enable conference calls and remote collaboration
- Trello – an application that enables the monitoring of a project with lists of tasks, comments, colour tagging and deadlines
- Evernote – a cloud-based project management tool that can be used to create 'to do' lists and enables you to manage your tasks effectively
- Slack – an application that enables people to interact throughout a project
- Gannt charts – software that allows you to plan and manage projects online, distribute tasks to a team, set deadlines and analyse progress

It is worth exploring some of these applications. Many have a web-based free or light version that you can practise using.

Time management skills are soft skills that can help you manage your time effectively. There is a wide range of tools and software that you can use to assist you. The aims of using time management tools are many, for example:

- establishing your goals
- organising your time

- producing an overview of tasks to complete
- setting deadlines
- prioritising your tasks
- coordinating with colleagues
- managing meetings
- enabling a focus on the job

You can use a variety of time management tools, such as a calendar, note-taking software and 'to do' lists. You can also train yourself to use various techniques to manage your time, for example using a Pomodoro timer or the Getting Things Done (GTD) application.

There is a lot of training in organisation, time and project management skills that is available either online or through your university. You can benefit from undertaking some training here in preparation for your work experience placement.

# Teamwork

The ability to work as part of a team is an essential quality in the media and creative industries as much of the project work is group-based. As with many of the other topics in this chapter, your key focus here is to transfer your university teamworking skills and qualities into the context of your placement. Consider some of the teamworking qualities you may already have exercised on your course:

- listening to and supporting others' ideas
- cooperating and working to a shared purpose
- showing initiative and making suggestions to others
- demonstrating motivation and completing delegated tasks in good time
- showing enthusiasm and encouraging enthusiasm in others
- adapting well to change

The following exercise will help you to reflect on your areas of strength in **teamwork** and how you can bring these to the workplace.

## Exercise: Developing Teamwork Qualities in the Workplace

In the table below, consider the teamworking qualities you already have and give examples of how you have exercised them during a group project on your course. Next, choose which areas you would like to bring into the workplace during your placement and list practical ways you can do this, for example, by speaking up in group meetings as a way of showing initiative. In the final column, make a note when you have exercised the chosen qualities during work experience. Keeping a record of your workplace achievements in this way means you can use it as evidence when you reflect on your placement.

| Teamworking quality | Example of how you have exercised this quality on a university project | Plan of how you might exercise this quality in the workplace |
|---|---|---|
| Listening to and supporting others' ideas | | |
| Cooperating and working to a shared purpose | | |
| Showing initiative and making suggestions to others | | |
| Demonstrating motivation and completing delegated tasks in good time | | |
| Showing enthusiasm and encouraging enthusiasm in others | | |
| Adapting well to change | | |

Follow up this exercise by observing the culture of the placement organisation in terms of teamwork. You can then model your approach accordingly.

# Communication and Interpersonal Skills

You will have a lot of experience of using and developing your **communication skills** and **interpersonal skills** while on your degree course. These are important skills to bring to the workplace. From composing a quick email to writing a detailed report, or from making a phone call to delivering a presentation, you can learn a lot from looking at your colleagues' written and spoken communication.

## Hear from the Experts

"Always let your employer know if you're not feeling well and if you don't think you can come to work. Get in touch by sending an email or a text, or give them a ring. Any decent employer will understand that if you're not very well, then you will need time off to recover. Keep your employer informed about your situation and they'll understand. Simple communication is the key!"

*– Tom Walters, Account Director, The Dairy*

"On work experience I'd always take cakes or biscuits! It gets the conversation going and you get to know people in that office. It's things like that which are small gestures, but they do make a big difference. And offer to make the tea! It won't get you a job, but it definitely shows that you've made an effort."

*– Emma Snow, Journalist, BBC*

"Sometimes students sit there for weeks and don't say much. I understand that it's a new environment with new people, so the experience can be a bit daunting, especially if you're working within a larger corporate setting. But at the same time, you want to make a good impression and you want to get the most out of it. Being silent for two weeks is not going to get you anywhere. Strike up a rapport with people. Believe in yourself, believe in your own ideas and thoughts. There's no such thing as a bad question or a bad idea. Shout up, speak up, and just have a go. We're quite a sociable bunch in marketing. We like to talk about the weather, what's on telly or what's going on in the world, so just talk about the things you would talk about with friends and family – we are normal people, I promise!"

*– Tom Walters, Account Director, The Dairy*

"How you conduct yourself on work experience is so important. Things like how you dress and how you interact with people create an immediate impression. It's important to show an interest – ask questions, but also know the right time to ask them! If a presenter or journalist is about to go on air or is in the middle of a breaking news story, it's probably best not to ask that question in that moment. Save it for later!"

*– Emma Snow, Journalist, BBC*

---

## Exercise: Observing Colleagues' Approach to Communication and Interpersonal Skills

Answer the following questions after observing your colleagues' approach to communication skills. This is an effective way of modelling your own professional behaviour in the workplace.

Communication skills:

- What evidence can you detect that active listening is taking place?
- How do colleagues demonstrate assertiveness?
- Can you identify examples when they use their negotiation skills?
- Write a summary of one of your colleague's management and leadership style

Written skills:

- What stylistic features of their writing makes it come across as professional?
- What tips can you pick up from their writing about them being aware of their audience and what they are wanting to achieve?
- List any technical language, jargon and acronyms that are in use and make sure you find out what all the terms mean

Spoken and presentation skills:

- Can you identify the purpose of the presentation? Who is the intended audience and what are they expected to do as a result of the presentation? Write a list of tips for yourself on how to deliver and present with confidence based on the techniques your colleagues use

Social media, web and networking skills:

*   How do your colleagues use professional social media in their work
*   What use do your colleagues make of the internet in their work? How do your colleagues use networking in their daily work?

Follow up the exercise by writing a list of tips and hints for yourself that detail what you have learned about effective communication in the workplace from your colleagues.

## Hear from the Experts

"Don't be afraid to ask questions. There's no such thing as a silly question. And become a sponge and absorb as much information as you can! Bring a notepad and a pen because there will be a lot of information that you can write down and remember for later. As an employer, we like interns who are prepared and proactive with note taking. Learn as much as you can from the people around you because your internship is an invaluable experience."

*– Tom Walters, Account Director, The Dairy*

"It's also important to conduct yourself in a professional manner. Be a nice person to be around and be helpful because that way, they're more likely to ask you back to freelance. Take notes as well, it's useful if you get asked back and it also shows you're willing to learn. I think that's really important."

*– Emma Snow, Journalist, BBC*

"Make new friends and be sociable. You could make friends for life. Make yourself irreplaceable in the mind of your employer. It's all about leaving a positive impression. We regularly attend networking opportunities or go for drinks in Nottingham, and we recently brought one of our interns with us because we knew that she would thrive in that kind of situation. She became really embedded within the team. If you are sociable, friendly and approachable, then your employer will be more likely to hand you those opportunities."

*– Tom Walters, Account Director, The Dairy*

# Personal Qualities

We will be referring here to Chapter 3 where we discovered what skills and qualities employers are looking for in potential employees.

Being on a placement gives you an ideal opportunity to model your professional behaviours in terms of how you convey your personal qualities. Personal qualities can include aspects such as how you present yourself to others, and your awareness of cultural and social diversity. The following information will set these out and signpost you to places where you can find extra information and support.

## Attendance, Punctuality and Reliability

You will be aware that attendance and punctuality are an important factor on your course, not only so that you don't miss out on your learning, but also so that you ensure you are contributing fully to team projects. Full attendance on a placement is important if you wish to get the most out of your work experience. It will also be expected by the placement provider. If you are working remotely or providing your services on a project to a set brief in a freelancing capacity, it is a good idea to keep a record of your own timekeeping, at least on a day-to-day basis.

Punctuality is often conflated or confused with attendance but refers specifically to being on time. Showing up early to the workplace in the morning or arriving early or on time to meetings is imperative if you want to give a good impression and demonstrate your keenness.

As Blalock (2013: 52) argues, '[t]he quality of reliability ... is a practical component of trust' and this can involve delivering a job on time, as well as demonstrating your punctuality as mentioned above. Your placement provider might be asked to comment on your reliability, so it is important that you build your brand of trustworthiness through dependability, promptness in responding, and faithfulness in follow-through' (Blalock, 2013, 52–53). Simple actions, such as responding quickly to emails or keeping to deadlines, are a good way of showcasing your reliability.

---

### Hear from the Expert

"[Punctuality] is a very basic piece of workplace etiquette, but it's one which is frankly the most important – be on time. At university you're expected to be on time for lectures, so you should be on time for work. Turning up late to your placement or your interview will only leave a bad impression. Come in early if you can, or at least make sure you allow more time to travel than you think you need, just in case you end up stuck in traffic, for example. There are days where things outside of your control will delay you and we understand that this will happen from time to time, but as a rule, be at work on time and don't make a habit of being late."

*– Tom Walters, Account Director, The Dairy*

---

## Multi-tasking, Adaptability and Flexibility

The personal qualities of multi-tasking, adaptability and flexibility encompass skills in time management as well as the ability to respond to instruction or to be adaptable if circumstances change at a given time. You will have experienced these qualities while on your course. At university, multi-tasking might involve working on several projects at once, but being able to prioritise which task needs completing first. Similarly, adaptability and flexibility might mean having to shelve one task temporarily in order to complete another deadline in good time.

While on your placement, demonstrate your adaptability by expecting the unexpected and show a willingness to be flexible. You can refer to the section above on organisation and time management to find useful digital applications to help you and make sure you keep a diary to note down all the tasks and deadlines that you are required to juggle.

## Enthusiasm and Positivity

It should almost go without saying that you will create a good impression on your place-ment if you demonstrate your enthusiasm and positivity in the workplace. You can do this partly through positive body language. Eggert (2010) has some simple tips to help you exude confidence and therefore display positivity: make eye contact, smile, keep your chin up, sit upright (don't slouch), and don't fidget. Eggert also recommends you breathe and walk slowly and drink plenty of water. These actions will not only help you to appear confident and positive, but will also keep you calm, reduce stress and assist your wellbeing (Eggert, 2010: 105). You can also demonstrate your enthusiasm by show-ing a genuine interest in the organisation and in the work you are doing. Your employer will appreciate it if you don't just wait to take orders, if you ask questions, are proactive and offer to help whenever it feels appropriate.

### Hear from the Experts

"Try not to doubt yourself. I think that's still advice I try to remind myself daily! For so long I struggled with imposter syndrome, I think because I was so young coming into the industry and I'm surrounded by people who have years of experience and are fantastic at what they do. I'm not sure imposter syndrome ever goes away. I know I'm not alone with that because I've spoken to my industry friends or people who have mentored me and have been in the busi-ness for years, and they still get waves of imposter syndrome! So, try not to overthink things and have a bit of belief. If you don't believe in yourself, then nobody will. It's taken me a long time to realise that."

*– Emma Snow, Journalist, BBC*

"You're constantly worried that someone's going to work you out and you're constantly scared that you're going to get caught pretending that you're doing this job. But the irony is, by doing that very thing, by working harder every day, you end up being able to do it. I never thought in a million years that I'd be owning my own agency 25 years after university. But the path has taken me this way because in the early stages of my career, I just grafted. I was accepting of criticism. I was very open to conversation because I didn't know what I was actually doing. I was actually quite open to asking people if I could improve. And through that series of adjust-ments throughout my career, I ended up becoming a director in that first agency. I ended up going to a national agency. And it was only then that I set up my own company, Framework Design.

*– Stephan Hayward, Managing Director, Framework Design*

## Self-discipline and a Sustained Commitment to a Shared Purpose

A sense of 'fitting in' can be an important goal for you during your work experience. Your aim is to feel part of the team rather than a token placement student who is there to observe as an 'outsider'. Showing commitment to a shared purpose is the best way to present yourself as a genuine colleague. Ask questions and find out what other people's roles are within the team to determine how your own skills and experience can best be utilised. You can improve your self-discipline by creating 'to do' lists, noting down deadlines and setting goals for each day rather than each week. Tick off your deadlines as you meet them, which will give you a sense of achievement.

### Hear from the Expert

"An internship is the start of your professional career. Just because you're still a student, doesn't mean that you have to think like a student. Think of yourself as an employee and think of this opportunity as a start of your professional journey. You're in the workplace, you're doing practical things, you're learning about the world of work – so get stuck in and become as involved in the business as you can because you will learn a lot more with a positive and professional attitude."

*– Tom Walters, Account Director, The Dairy*

## Resilience and Assertiveness

The World Economic Forum's *The Future of Jobs Report 2020* lists 'resilience, stress tolerance and flexibility' as one of the top ten categories of skills for 2025, which suggests its importance as a crucial personal quality in the workplace (World Economic Forum, 2020). **Resilience** might simply be defined as having the ability to overcome setbacks and recover quickly from difficulties. There will undoubtedly be some challenges that arise from any new situation, and it would be unusual not to have to face some challenges while on your placement. The key thing here is to accept them as learning experiences that you can build on. You can learn how to understand and make the most of your natural strengths and are advised to work with colleagues in a positive and productive manner. Sharing your day-to-day experiences of being on placement with your work colleagues, fellow students and your tutor will deter feelings of isolation and give you an opportunity to discuss any challenges you may be facing. ScreenSkills (screenskills.com) offers online training courses in resilience for its members. It is worth signing up for membership because some of these courses are free. Additionally, your course and the careers service will offer support and training in these areas.

## Self-awareness and Emotional Intelligence

**Self-awareness** and **emotional intelligence** are useful qualities to exercise in the workplace. Being self-aware and understanding how others might see you or interpret your actions enables you to behave appropriately in professional situations. Daniel Goleman (2004) lists five features of emotional intelligence:

- self-awareness – the ability to understand your own strengths and weaknesses
- self-regulation – the ability to think before acting, being open to change and having the ability to say 'no'
- internal motivation – a genuine reason or passion for behaving or acting in a particular way; having the ability to defer immediate results for the benefit of receiving long-term gains
- social skills – the personal skills needed for successful communication and interaction; being good at building and maintaining relationships
- empathy – the ability to understand the feelings of others

Considering how you may come across to others in the workplace is a useful gauge for modelling your behaviour from being a student to becoming a professional. Consider what strengths you have that you can offer to your placement provider, endeavour to interact well with colleagues and build a working relationship in which they see you as a motivated and dependable team member.

## Honesty and Maturity

Exercising your emotional intelligence is also a way of demonstrating your honesty and maturity in a workplace context. While undertaking work experience, you will want to give your placement provider and colleagues a good impression of yourself. Creating a positive atmosphere in the workplace will give you personal fulfilment and help you to enjoy your time on the placement. It will also bring you further rewards later. Positive feedback and testimonials from the placement provider will boost your confidence. It will also potentially provide you with material to reflect on in a placement report or essay and to add to your professional social media.

A placement provider can be an appropriate person to ask for a reference when looking for further work. Typical characteristics that potential employers ask referees to comment on are honesty and maturity, so it is important that you can demonstrate these qualities in a professional context. Be honest about what skills you have to offer the placement provider from the experience you have gained on your course, but also let them know about any areas you would like to improve on during the placement – after all, you are there to learn and gain experience. How you present yourself and respond to others in situations like this will display your levels of maturity.

---

**Hear from the Experts**

"Don't disregard a task, project or experience. Even if you think you're not particularly skilled at something, give it a go. You're there to learn and the employer will understand that you won't know everything. We don't expect you to be a fully qualified marketing professional because you're on a placement, so try and have a go at as many different things as you can."

*– Tom Walters, Account Director, The Dairy*

"Smile and offer to make a tea. Sounds really cliche, but it works. Just offer to be helpful. There is a balance, though. Don't badger people every 20 minutes. You might have an hour or two where you're doing nothing. Just try and look busy. Find that balance between saying I can do that, I can help, but also not being a real pain in the neck! I would suggest just be yourself."

*– Dick Stone, Broadcast Consultant*

---

# Mental Health Awareness in the Workplace

Working in the media and creative industries is rewarding and exciting, but it can also be stressful. Hasson and Butler (2020) offer advice for supporting yourself to stay well at work, and you can begin to foster these habits while on your placement:

- Breathe – concentrate on your breathing. Breathe through your nose to the count of 4, hold it for a count of 7, then slowly exhale through your mouth to a count of 8. Repeat until you feel calmer
- Get active – use any opportunity you have to get some exercise by walking part of the way to your placement or taking breaks at lunchtime to go for a walk
- Seek out nature – organise your day, week or weekend so that you can spend some time in a green space, such as a park. You can even incorporate this into your lunch break walk
- Eat well – enjoy a balanced diet, stay hydrated by drinking two litres of water a day, and avoid taking in too much caffeine and alcohol
- Sleep well – keep a regular sleep pattern and minimise your use of phones and computers before bedtime
- Manage social media – while working, limit your use of social media applications to avoid distractions
- Connection to others – keep in touch with your friends and family to avoid feelings of isolation. It is a great idea, for example, to keep in touch with other people on your course and offer each other support while on placement

(adapted from Hasson and Butler, 2020: 78–84)

ScreenSkills offers guidance to members on how to support your own wellbeing as well as advice on how you can help to support your colleagues (ScreenSkills, n.d. screenskills. com/training/work-ready-skills/transferable-competencies/mental-health-awareness/).

# Awareness of Cultural and Social Diversity

Our final example of professional behaviour to demonstrate during your placement is your **cultural awareness** and awareness of social **diversity**. During your degree course you will have looked at issues of representation in the media as part of your theoretical modules and you are encouraged to consider these issues when working on practical projects. As with some of the other professional qualities discussed in this chapter, you are encouraged to transfer your knowledge and experience into a workplace context.

You can do some research into Equality, Diversity and Inclusion (EDI), or undertake some training prior to your placement to help practise your cultural awareness. It is worthwhile becoming a member of ScreenSkills so you can access their online learning pages. Their *Work Well* modules include some useful information on wellbeing in the workplace as well as awareness of unconscious bias, harassment and bullying, and Equality, Diversity and Inclusion.

You may wish to do some research in other areas from the organisations listed below. Demonstrating your awareness of some of these areas to placement providers and potential future employers will stand you in good stead for the future.

- Creative Diversity Network (CDN) (creativediversitynetwork.com) – this network has high-profile broadcasting companies as members, including the BBC, ITV, Sky, S4C and BAFTA. CDN captures diversity and inclusion data and supports the UK broadcasting industry so that it understands the diversity and inclusion landscape. Their website offers helpful advice on how organisations can build a diversity and inclusion strategy and provides examples of strategies from the BBC, Sky and ITV.
- GLAAD (glaad.org) – this American media-monitoring organisation (formerly known as the Gay and Lesbian Alliance Against Defamation) provides a very useful online reference guide for journalists and other media creators to assist them in telling stories of LGBTQ people 'fairly and accurately'. They are careful to point out that there is 'no one way to be LGBTQ, nor is there one way to describe LGBTQ people', and for this reason good practice is to ask people how they describe themselves and what their pronouns are (glaad.org/reference). The reference guide is a valuable tool for media producers in finding a fair language for their work. It includes a glossary of LGBTQ and transgender terms.
- Pact (diversity.pact.co.uk) – Pact is a trade association committed to improving diversity within the media industry. Its website has information on understanding equality law, tackling unconscious bias, and how to write an equality and diversity policy for organisations. These may be a useful resource for your research into cultural and social diversity.
- TripleC (triplec.org.uk) – this is an organisation for deaf, disabled and neurodivergent people to improve their access to the arts and media industries.

Its guidelines for disability inclusion in UK television production, entitled *The 5 As*, supports organisations to:

○ Anticipate – that they will be working with disabled people on a regular basis

○ Ask – invite team members to discuss adjustment or access requirements

○ Assess – regularly evaluate and improve inclusion policies and practices

○ Adjust – put in place any reasonable adjustment to ensure full inclusion and the physical and emotional wellbeing of Disabled talent

○ Advocate – celebrate what Disabled talent bring and actively champion them

(summarised from *The 5 As*, triplec.org.uk/wp-content/uploads/2022/10/The-5-As_ FINAL_230822.pdf)

It will be a useful resource to raise your awareness of how deaf, disabled and neurodivergent people can be supported in accessing the arts and media and to build your awareness of cultural and social diversity. TripleC also run events, masterclasses and workshops through their Disabled Artists Networking Community (DANC). You can sign up for e-newsletters from DANC via the TripleC webpages.

• Women in Film and Television UK (wftv.org.uk) – this is a membership organisation for women working in creative media in the UK and form part of an international network. The WFTV resource hub has information on anti-bullying and harassment, anti-racism, disability and accessibility, and wellbeing. You can access these resources (for free) as part of your research into what it is like for women working in film and television. WFTV also run a regular events programme in person and online for members. Membership requires payment, but once you have enrolled the events programme is free.

You can also investigate some of the sector networks and support organisations we listed in Chapter 2 to see what online guidance and training they offer to members and non-members. There is a wealth of information to discover from these organisations and you may wish to return to this list once you graduate.

## Creativity and Innovation

Employers are increasingly seeking **creativity and innovation** in their employees. The World Economic Forum's *The Future of Jobs Report 2020* identifies creativity and innovation among the top ten skills for 2025 (World Economic Forum, 2020). This skillset includes a focus on analytical thinking and innovation, critical thinking, analysis and creativity, originality, and initiative. It does not just apply to people working in the creative sector, but is important for employees in many areas. Creativity in this context is about being able to offer new ideas and solutions to challenges. It is about looking at things from different and unique angles. Innovation is about putting those ideas into action.

Displaying creativity and innovation on your placement will enable you to make a difference to the organisation, and in turn display your **commercial sector awareness**. You will already have well-developed creativity and innovation skills from your degree course, but these are also workplace skills that you can develop and improve on while on placement. You can do this by focusing on:

- practising **mindfulness** to aid your creativity (see the earlier section in this chapter on mental health awareness in the workplace)
- being inquisitive and open minded and showing a willingness to learn
- being open to change and making connections
- being aware of your working environment and making it conducive to creativity
- being confident, taking risks and taking the plunge
- being committed to your own idea/s and seeing them through
- utilising a variety of techniques for generating ideas, such as mind-mapping

You can undertake some training on creativity and innovation to prepare you for your placement. Courses are available online via LinkedIn and other providers, and your university may also offer training sessions. Search for courses with titles such as 'Develop Your Creative Thinking and Innovation Skills', 'Fostering Innovation' and 'Creativity Boot Camp' to find appropriate training materials.

### Exercise: Identifying Evidence of Creativity and Innovation

Identify and list examples, and provide evidence, of your creativity and innovation. It can be from your university course or your wider life. Think about a time when you have found a creative solution to a problem or found a new way to approach something. Think about how you can apply this experience to your work placement.

# Supervision and Support

We have suggested in previous sections of this chapter that you observe your colleagues' behaviour in the workplace. You are likely to have a main supervisor while on placement and they will probably be responsible for providing you with support, supervision and feedback. Another workplace skill that is good for you to hone is the ability to give and receive feedback. Being open to constructive suggestions from your supervisor and other colleagues will serve you well while on placement.

You are advised to seek out support throughout your placement. Support can be in the form of a formal appraisal meeting or something a little more casual, such as short, regular catch-up meetings. Whatever way support is organised on your placement, you can prepare for it in various ways. It is worth getting into the habit of seeking and receiving feedback. It will give you the opportunity to hear, understand and respond to things that will help improve your performance in the role. It will also help you gauge whether you are meeting the expectations of your placement provider.

Don't be shy about asking for advice and feedback while you are on placement as it is a good way of learning from the work experience. Seeking feedback can also ensure you are progressing in the role. You may want feedback on your performance, a specific task or skill, or on a deliverable that you are working on. You should seek feedback from your placement supervisor but you can also ask for advice from colleagues. Give them an idea of what you would like feedback on and let them know that you are open to their advice. Think about what you hope to gain from any feedback and prepare some notes and questions in advance. Try to find the right time for having a feedback meeting, when there are few interruptions and the setting is relaxed.

When it comes to receiving feedback, take account of the following suggestions:

- be open and aware of your use of body language and tone of voice, and approach feedback with an open and positive mind
- listen carefully to the feedback without interrupting and try to avoid being defensive. Don't feel pressurised to show agreement or disagreement or to offer excuses and explanations
- try to hear and understand what the person offering the feedback is saying, but also what the intention behind the feedback is. Try to show that you understand what is being said
- repeat back the feedback to ensure you have understood, making notes of the main points
- take your time to react to feedback and ask for more information or clarification if necessary
- reflect on the feedback in a constructive way and explain what or how you are planning to change and improve
- learn how to improve from any feedback you receive
- seek out further feedback on a regular basis
- see this feedback as an opportunity to develop and improve

# Conclusion

In this chapter we have given you some advice on how to get the best out of your work experience, including how to model your professional behaviour in the workplace. We have worked through several functional skills that will help you be effective in your work experience. You can use this to inform your approach to the workplace and as the basis of reflecting on your work experience, which is the focus of the next chapter.

## Further Reading

Blalock, Becky (2013) *Dare: Straight Talk on Confidence, Courage, and Career for Women in Charge*. London: John Wiley and Sons. This book offers advice to women on how to break the glass ceiling. You can look through some of the early chapters for inspiration on how to gain confidence in the workplace.

Eggert, Max (2010) *Body Language: Impress, Persuade and Succeed with the Power of Body Language*. London: Pearson Education. This is a useful guide. Chapter 8 provides tips and hints about how to express personal confidence through body language.

Goleman, Daniel (2004) *Emotional Intelligence and Working with Emotional Intelligence*. London: Bloomsbury. This is a useful text for deepening your understanding about emotional intelligence in the workplace.

Hasson, Gill, and Butler, Donna (2020) *Mental Health and Wellbeing in the Workplace: A Practical Guide for Employers and Employees*. London: John Wiley and Sons. This book offers practical advice on how to maintain mental health and wellbeing in the workplace.

TripleC (n.d.) *The 5As, Guidelines for Disability Inclusion in UK Television Production* (triplec.org.uk/wp-content/uploads/2022/10/The-5-As_FINAL_230822.pdf). This is a document to ensure the full and equal inclusion of Deaf, Disabled and/or Neurodivergent talent, both behind and in front of the camera.

# 12

# REFLECTING ON WORK EXPERIENCE

## Debriefing and Critical Reflection

## Introduction

In the previous chapter we discussed the importance of developing a range of work-based skills. In this chapter we will support you as you reflect on your placement, but also more generally on any work experience you do. In particular, this chapter will enable you to contemplate your work experience before moving on to make the important search for **graduate employment**.

The aims and outcomes of this chapter are:

- to debrief on the successful and less successful elements of your work experience and how to learn from these
- to obtain a reference from an employer/placement provider
- to learn how to write a work experience report and a critically reflective essay
- to update your professional branding in response to your work experience

List of exercises in this chapter:

- Debriefing after the placement
- Producing a reflective report on work experience
- Writing a critical reflection essay on work experience
- Updating your professional branding

## First Steps to Writing Your Report: The Debriefing

The intention of this chapter is to guide you through the production of a reflective report on your work experience. The exercise below will be your first step in researching and generating content for your report. It is recommended that you do this exercise when you feel ready to start the report, which is usually once you have completed your placement/work experience activity. If you have been keeping a reflective diary and making a record of your placement tasks and duties, as well as how you felt throughout the placement, you will already have a lot of notes to refer to when you start writing.

Let's try to break down your experiences of the placement by starting with a **debriefing**. A debriefing is useful because it can help you to refer back to your placement aims and help you analyse whether you achieved those aims, and also how you feel about them. It may be that you are pleased with your achievements in some areas, but in others you feel there may be room for improvement. Your placement is a continuous learning experience and reflecting on what you have learned will provide you with content for the report.

## Exercise: Debriefing After the Placement

The following table comprises a list of statements from students who have previously been on placement. They cover a variety of areas, from applying theory to practice, to assessing your personal qualities, the use of your skills, the work culture, your interpersonal skills and any specialist skills you may have acquired.

Select the statements that apply to your experience and think about what they tell you about your experience and what you have learned about yourself on your placement. You can also add your own statements if your experiences are not covered here. What do you notice about your selection? Are you recognising any patterns? Can you identify your strengths and weaknesses? Can you recognise some statements as being more important than others in relation to your professional development? Record your initial thoughts about your choices and why you have selected these statements. These statements and your thoughts about them will provide the main body of your report, so you can refer to them and elaborate on them when you write your report.

| | | | |
|---|---|---|---|
| The placement helped me realise I need to get more of an insight and find out what opportunities are open to me in the sector | The placement made me realise that I could look for more opportunities to produce work for my professional portfolio | The placement helped me realise I would benefit from gaining more experience relevant to my future career that I can cite on my CV | The placement helped me realise I need to develop my teamwork and interpersonal skills further |
| The placement helped me realise I need to build my networks and networking skills further | The placement helped me realise I need to boost my self-confidence, resilience, and awareness of the importance of mental health and wellbeing in the workplace | The placement helped me realise that I can apply theory from my degree to practice in the real world | The placement helped me realise there is a variety of different types of work cultures and organisations that I could enter |

*(Continued)*

| | | | |
|---|---|---|---|
| The placement helped me realise I would benefit from improving and developing my problem-solving skills further | The placement helped me realise I would benefit from being a little more proactive, flexible, showing a positive attitude and a 'can-do' approach | The placement helped me realise I might benefit from demonstrating my motivation and dedication more often | The placement helped me realise I could improve my communication skills |
| The placement helped me realise I need to improve my technical skills and would benefit from learning to use these in a work context | The placement helped me realise I could do more to demonstrate my level of creativity and use my creative skills in a professional context | The placement helped me realise I could do with improving my project management, time management and organisational skills further | The placement helped me realise the importance of my developing cultural awareness (in relation to equality, diversity and inclusion) in the workplace |

# Placement Feedback/Employer Reference

It is important to gain feedback from your employer/placement provider. Feedback can provide useful content for your report and for your CV when applying for work. Feedback provides evidence of good performance, but it can also include indicators of where you need to improve. Feedback can be in the form of a reference or a testimonial from your placement provider. Your placement provider or employer may have a pre-existing reference form for giving feedback, but if they don't, you can ask for feedback on some of the following aspects of your performance, depending on what you, your employer and your university tutor think is appropriate:

- quality of work produced
- attendance and punctuality
- contribution to the organisation
- confidence and resilience
- ability to follow a brief
- cultural awareness (for example, equality, diversity and inclusion awareness, sustainability awareness)
- teamwork and interpersonal skills demonstrated
- networking skills demonstrated
- motivation and dedication
- ability to work independently
- positivity, proactivity, flexibility
- problem-solving skills displayed
- communication skills displayed
- organisational and project management skills demonstrated
- level of creativity

- technical skills applied to the workplace
- time management skills

# Reflecting on Work Experience

So far in this chapter we have helped you to collate information about your work experience to reflect on. It comprises your own personal opinion and the feedback provided by the placement provider. You are now ready to start writing a reflective report.

Writing a reflective report is a useful exercise for three reasons. First, it helps you to organise your thoughts about the placement and to reflect on them. Second, it is something that you can refer back to and use parts of when you apply for future work. The content can help to inform supporting statements in applications, for example. It can also help to prepare you for interviews. Third, it gives you the experience of report writing, which is itself a very useful skill in the workplace.

You can produce your work experience reflection as a formal written report, as we do in the following exercise, or as a blog, vlog or podcast.

Report writing at its very best is focused, succinct, and uses evidence and specific examples to support the arguments and statements you make in the report. Again, this is a useful skill that can be applied when writing job applications and during job interviews. For example, there is no point in saying you can think on your feet if you do not provide a specific example of an occasion when you did this. The specific examples provide context for your statements.

A checklist of criteria that you should aim for when writing the report includes:

- evidence of the quality and success of the placement
- evidence of career skills developed from the placement
- evidence of critical reflection on the work experience
- evidence of setting out aims for future development

# Reflective Writing for a Work Experience Report

In order to successfully and meaningfully evaluate your work experience you are encouraged to use the following structure to take you from pure description to deep reflection:

- describe a situation that happened
- describe the outcome of what happened
- discuss your response to what happened, and the reactions of others
- think about the event in the light of prior learning experiences, think about how you might have approached the situation differently
- say how this would have affected the outcome
- explain what you have learned from the experience and how it will influence your future approach in a similar situation

(adapted from Moon, 2004)

Because you are writing from personal experience, you can use straightforward, non-academic language and refer to yourself in the first person, for example, 'I think...', 'I felt...', 'I realised...'.

The primary audience for your report is your university tutor (if it is for course work). You could also use this report as a way of demonstrating your career development learning to your placement provider or future employers, so they may be the secondary audience for the report.

## Exercise: Producing a Reflective Report on Work Experience

We will now provide a step-by-step guide of what you can include in the placement report and how you might structure it. We will break the report down into sections and offer suggestions, advice and examples for each one. Remember, we are only making suggestions and giving examples. Your report will undoubtedly have your own individual touch.

## Title Page

Suggestions for the title page are:

- a title for your report, such as: 'a reflective report on work experience with ... [insert name of placement provider]'
- your name and student details
- the date when the report was written
- graphics and images to illustrate the cover page which are relevant to the content of the report. For example, a collage of images that reflect the experience or placement-providing organisation (you can insert graphics and illustrations throughout the report where appropriate)

## Contents Page

The contents page is an outline of the structure of the report. It should fit on one page and cannot be created until you have finished the rest of the report. We suggest the following:

- list the different sections of the report (which we will cover below), which should be numbered, along with the page numbers on which they can be found. You can create hyperlinks from the contents list to the different sections of the report
- include a list of the appendices, including the full title of each (for example, 'Appendix 1: Placement details')

The figure below sets out an example of a contents page.

| A Reflective Report on Work Experience as a Runner with XX Productions | |
| --- | --- |
| **Contents Page** | |
| 1.0 Introduction | Page 1 |
| 2.0 Main Body | |
| 2.1 Academic learning | Page 2 |
| 2.2 Personal qualities | Page 3 |
| 2.3 Work culture | Page 4 |
| 2.4 Interpersonal skills | Page 5 |
| 2.5 Specialist skills | Page 7 |
| 2.6 Generic/transferable skills | Page 8 |
| 2.7 Making a difference | Page 10 |
| 3.0 Conclusions | Page 11 |
| 4.0 Recommendations | Page 12 |
| 5.0 Appendices | Page 13 |
| 5.1 Appendix 1: Details of work experience undertaken | |
| 5.2 Appendix 2: Log/timeline of the work experience | |
| 5.3 Appendix 3: Work experience blog | |
| 5.4 Appendix 4: Reference/recommendation/testimonial | |
| 5.5 Appendix 5: Evidence of arranging the work experience | |
| 5.6 Appendix 6: Examples of work completed | |
| 5.7 Appendix 7: Photos from the work experience | |

## Introduction

This section is an introduction to and summary of the report. It can be as little as one page long. The best advice is to write your introduction once the bulk of the report is written, as you will then have a good idea of the form your report has taken.

The introduction should be a brief description of what you did for your work experience, including the details of your placement provider, and where and when your work experience took place. Discuss your aims and objectives for the report and tell the reader what they are going to read.

Summarise the main objectives that you hoped your work experience would provide. You can use the SMART objectives you identified in the exercise in Chapter 6 to help with this.

## Main Body

This is the main content of the report and follows a set of suggested sub-headings (see below). This is where you will elaborate on your reflections from the debriefing exercise at the beginning of the chapter. You are advised to keep a blog to record the experience whilst on placement. You can add quotes from your blog in the main body of the report to serve as examples and evidence for some of your reflections. You can also quote from any references, testimonials and feedback you have received from your work experience provider to use as evidence in the main body of your report.

## Main Body – Sub-section 1: Academic Learning

The first paragraph should discuss how your work experience has enabled you to make connections with your degree course content. For example, you can discuss how you have been able to apply theory to practice in the working environment. You may want to point to specific examples of modules, and where and how the subject and course materials have been of value to your work experience.

## Main Body – Sub-section 2: Personal Qualities

In this section you may want to consider whether and how your work experience has helped to boost your self-confidence, resilience and awareness of the importance of mental health and wellbeing in the workplace. You can also discuss how your proactivity, positivity and flexibility has been developed. Include here any areas that have been highlighted through your work experience as needing further development or improvement. You can refer to Chapters 10 and 11 where we discussed some of these themes.

## Main Body – Sub-section 3: Work Culture

This section requires a consideration of how the work experience has increased your understanding of how different organisations function and are structured, and the relative benefits of different work cultures. Examples of different work cultures are a 9–5 office job, a shoot on location, and remote working with online meetings. You should discuss how the work culture impacted on your approach to the job and what sort of work culture you aspire to in future.

## Main Body – Sub-section 4: Interpersonal Skills

This section requires you to analyse and reflect on whether and how the work experience has enabled you to develop. You can provide evidence from your experience to demonstrate your interpersonal skills, such as teamwork, social skills, communication skills and cultural awareness, along with your leadership, management and networking skills.

## Main Body – Sub-section 5: Specialist Skills

This section encourages you to analyse whether and how the work experience has helped you demonstrate and develop your specialist skills. These are skills specific to the job role, such as digital media marketing skills, technical media skills, production skills, and creative, communication and research skills.

## Main Body – Sub-section 6: Generic/Transferable Skills

This section is about whether and how the work experience has helped you to use and improve skills that can be transferred to other workplace contexts. It can include skills such as problem-solving, time management and project management.

## Main Body – Sub-section 7: Making a Difference

In this section you can consider what difference you made to the organisation you worked with. This links to the idea that when approaching potential employers, you are advised to tell them what *you* can offer them, not what they can do for you. You can also discuss what difference the organisation has made to you, especially in terms of gaining an insight into the sector.

## Drawing Conclusions

Use this section to detail the conclusions you have reached from your work experience placement. In other words, you should discuss what you have learned as a result of undertaking the work experience.

## Making Recommendations

For this section you should discuss some recommendations or 'notes to self' about how you will action the conclusions you have drawn (above) from your work experience. Your recommendations should be SMART, that is specific, measurable, achievable, realistic/relevant and time-bound. Your recommendations can focus on the following aspects: making links with your degree course, enhancing your personal qualities and awareness of the sector, developing your skills and qualities, building your networks and getting more experience.

## Appendices

The material that supports the content of the report, and is evidence of the points you have made in the main body, is included in the appendices. Include only material you think the reader will need or want to know about and do not introduce new information here. You should refer to each appendix somewhere in the main body of the report. The appendix can be as long as you wish, as long as the material is relevant and referred to in the main body of the report. Each appendix should be labelled in the following style: 'Appendix 1: Details of work experience undertaken'.

Below is a selection of the sorts of appendices that you can include in your report.

## Appendix 1: Details of Work Experience Undertaken

This appendix can contain information about the organisation you worked with. It can include a screen shot and link to their website, company reports, information about your placement supervisor (such as a LinkedIn profile, their position within the organisation, or similar).

## Appendix 2: Log/Timeline of the Work Experience

This appendix can contain a timeline or log of what you did and when during your work experience.

## Appendix 3: Work Experience Blog

This appendix is a blog of the work experience, describing and reflecting on what you did and how you felt. You should paste a link to your blog here. You can quote directly from it in the main body of the report to provide evidence of the points you have made.

## Appendix 4: Reference/Recommendation/Testimonial

This appendix is where you can record any kind of feedback you received during your work experience. This can be through a formal reference, recommendation or testimonial, or through more informal channels. It may be useful to quote from this feedback in the main body of your report.

## Appendix 5: Evidence of Arranging the Work Experience

This appendix contains material detailing the setting up of the work experience, such as emails/messages between you and the placement provider, the job advert you responded to, the CV and cover letter you used to apply for it, any evidence of an interview for the placement if you had one. Other evidence of how you set up more general work experience (such as working on a live brief or volunteering) can also go here.

## Appendix 6: Examples of Work Completed

This appendix can include examples of what you actually did while on work experience. It can include copies of workstreams, briefings and content produced, such as videos, press releases and blogs. It is important that you ensure you have the necessary permissions to include such work in your report. Any permissions should be in writing and included in this appendix.

## Appendix 7: Photos from the Work Experience

You can include photos taken while you were on your work experience in this appendix. For example, a collage of photos of you in the work context. Note that you must gain written permission from the people in any photos you take and include it in the appendix.

## Exercise: Writing a Critical Reflection Essay on Work Experience

As an alternative to writing a report, you can choose to focus on a specific aspect of your work experience and write about it in the form of a critically reflective essay. Choose a title from the list below:

- Explain how one of the following interpersonal skills was used during your work experience: teamwork; social skills; communication skills; leadership and management
- Analyse how you were able to apply theory from your degree course content to practice in the workplace
- Examine the importance of networking and your strategies for future career development
- Explore the personal qualities that you found to be important to your work experience
- Consider the importance of work culture to your future career choices
- Discuss how your developing cultural awareness was reinforced by your work experience, for example, through equality, diversity, and inclusion (EDI)
- The World Economic Forum, *The Future of Jobs Report 2020* (2020: 36), identifies 'Creativity, originality and initiative' as a top skill for the employees of the future. Reflecting on your own work experience explain how this is an essential skill for future employees. Explore your future specialist skills training needs as they emerged during your work experience
- Discuss the effect of your work experience on developing your confidence and resilience, and why it is important for your future
- Reflecting on your work experience, how did you make a difference to your placement provider/organisation, and what difference did it make for you?

# Updating Your Professional Branding After Work Experience

Now that you have reflected on your work experience and considered the feedback you have received on your placement, it is an appropriate time to review your professional branding. Consider how you can update your professional branding in light of your work experience. The following exercise will guide you.

## Exercise: Updating your Professional Branding

Use the checklist below to identify areas of your existing professional branding that you can now update in light of your work experience. You may also wish to create new channels to showcase your professional brand as a result of your work experience.

- CV – add details of your latest placement to the list of relevant work experience on your CV. Detail the job description and explain your main duties. Add examples of the key skills you have developed through your placement to your key skills list. Consider asking your placement provider if they would be willing to act as one of your referees for future jobs

- LinkedIn profile – add details of your work experience to your LinkedIn profile. In your headline, indicate the role or area of work in which you have experience. Can you add any new certificates or qualifications to it? Do you need a new professional head shot? Would your placement employer be willing to provide you with a recommendation?
- Portfolio/website – update and add your work experience to your portfolio/ website. You may want to focus on adding examples of work created to your showreel and adding testimonials/recommendations from your placement employer
- Video sharing sites – YouTube, Vimeo and TikTok. Update these to include any new content you have created. Link or embed videos to your portfolio/website
- Professional blog/vlog – update your professional blog/vlog by posting your reflections about your work experience
- ScreenSkills – update your profile with details of your work experience
- IMDb – if you have produced any film work for your work experience, add the details to your IMDb profile
- Other social media – Twitter/X, Instagram, Facebook, The Dots and other professional social media accounts. You should add images from your work experience to these accounts and update your biographical details. For the latter, you can name a specific role that you feel you are suited to (for example, photographer, director of photography, copywriter, communications assistant)

Having added details of your recent work experience across all your branding, think about the key messages you are communicating about yourself as a future creative professional. For example if you are identifying yourself as particularly skilled in camera work you can foreground this by calling yourself a Director of Photography (DoP). Another example might be for you to demonstrate the amount of work experience you have had by listing it on your professional social media accounts.

# Conclusion

We have come to the end of this chapter about analysing and reflecting on your work experience. The exercises will have helped you to organise your thoughts and experiences having completed your work experience placement, and prepared you for writing a report or a critically reflective essay. Your report will be a very useful tool that you can refer to when looking for future employment. It will remind you of your achievements and give you plenty of evidence and examples that you can refer to in job applications and interviews.

In the next chapter we will focus on preparing for graduation by assisting you in the creation of a career plan.

## Further Reading

Edwards, Julian (2022) *Write Reflectively*. London: Sage. This 'quick skills' guide is a useful reference for finding a structure and writing style to communicate your experiences.

Kerry, Matthew, and Stone, Georgia (2018) *Introducing Media Practice: The Essential Guide*. London: Sage. Chapter 11 of this book provides guidance on reflective writing and writing a reflective report.

Moon, Jenny (2004) *A Handbook of Reflective and Experiential Learning: Theory and Practice*. London: Routledge. Moon's book offers some helpful techniques and approaches to writing in a critically reflective way. You may find it useful for further guidance before writing your report or essay.

# 13

# PREPARING FOR GRADUATION

## Setting Out Your Career Plan

## Introduction

In the previous two chapters, we focused on the process of carrying out and reflecting on your work experience. In this concluding chapter, we are going to start looking forward in more detail to your graduation and the preparations for planning your future career after leaving university.

This chapter will support you in writing a **career plan**. It will outline the benefits of having a plan and provide a step-by-step guide to help you create it.

The aims and outcomes of this chapter are to help you develop a strategy for your career plan by doing the following:

- assessing your skills and interests
- setting career goals
- developing a plan of action

Having reached this stage in the book you will have already created a lot of material from researching media and creative industries websites, industry reports, job listings, and from your interviews with employees in the industry. You are encouraged to refer back to this material to help inform the content of your career plan wherever it is relevant.

## What is a Career Plan?

Your career plan will provide you with a record of all the research you have done so far in formulating a plan for your future career. It will be a useful repository for listing your career preferences, jobs you might apply for, the skills and interests you have, the synopsis of your education and qualifications, a copy of your CV and cover letter/email, and references, for example. Once it is completed, the career plan will be invaluable to you when you are searching for and applying for jobs. It will help to keep you inspired and will also be a place to find all the important resources you have collated while working through this book.

You may be planning to work for yourself or to combine working for an employer with some freelance work. In either case, it is recommended that you create a career plan with self-employment in mind.

First, we will provide a checklist of the career plan contents. Then we will include some further guidance on how to go about finding information for the career plan.

# Format of the Career Plan

It is recommended that you produce your career plan as a portfolio, using any software you prefer (Word or PowerPoint, for instance). At this stage, it is worth setting up your portfolio in whatever form you choose and creating the pages/slides with a heading on each in the order given in the table below. This is to ensure that you can retrieve information and resources quickly and easily.

You should start by choosing what career area you want to focus your career plan on. This may be the area you researched for the career case study in Chapter 4. If you now feel you want to look in a different direction, revisit Chapter 2 where you investigated the media and creative industries, and Chapter 5 if you are interested in freelancing or self-employment.

Once you have decided on your career focus, start to flesh out information about this in your career plan.

Use the following checklist to organise the content of your career plan. It should contain the following information:

| Title page | |
| --- | --- |
| **Title of pages/slides** | **Description of content of pages/slides** |
| Career preferences | Describe and analyse your career aspirations in terms of what type of career would suit you, including salary level, work culture and future career progression |
| Jobs shortlist | Decide on a shortlist of job titles or freelance opportunities and list some keywords that are relevant to your career aspirations |
| Places of work | State where in the world you would like to work, e.g. which country, county or city. List your preferences and give reasons |
| Potential employers | List some employers and organisations you would like to work with and say why each one appeals to you. For self-employment, you could find a business that you would like to emulate and state your reasons |
| Key messages | Decide on some key messages that you want to give about yourself to employers or clients (if you intend to work for yourself). Include messages about your experience, your skills, your personality and your unique selling point |

**Title page**

| Title of pages/slides | Description of content of pages/slides |
| --- | --- |
| Sources for job adverts | Research and list sources for jobs adverts that link to your particular job search, e.g. LinkedIn, company websites, networks and job websites |
| Examples of jobs | Include screen shots of some live jobs (advert, job description, person specification) that you think you could apply for on graduating from your degree. If working for yourself, look for examples of potential clients or freelance opportunities |
| Further study | Give details of any further study you intend to engage in, such as postgraduate courses, vocational industry accredited courses, training schemes and apprenticeships |

Pages/slides on what you have to offer. The next thing to do is to think about yourself in terms of your future career. You should flesh out the following information:

| | |
| --- | --- |
| Interests, skills, and strengths | Describe and analyse these in relation to your future career. These should be from your education, life experience, hobbies, extra-curricular and work experience so far |
| Education | Write a summary of your education to date and evaluate how you will use this to contribute to your future career |
| Work experience | Give a summary of your experience of work to date and how this will contribute to your career going forward |

Pages/slides on your career materials. In this section you should review and refine your resources for making job applications

| | |
| --- | --- |
| CV and cover letter/email | Include a revised copy of your template CV and draft cover letter/email |
| Referees | Decide on the referees to name on your CV and gain their permission. Prepare notes on what you would like them to mention in their reference for you. Do the same for any testimonials/recommendations that you might use on your online portfolio or professional social media |
| Professional branding | Include links to the professional social media and online portfolios, websites and blogs that you have developed |

Pages/slides linked to networking

| | |
| --- | --- |
| Your networks | Review your potential networks for jobs, such as work experience employers, alumni of your degree course and contacts via your professional social media accounts. List these and detail how they might be able to help you to gain future employment |
| Networking | Look out for networking events, careers fairs and employer presentations. Add details of these here |
| Elevator pitch | Include a copy of your elevator pitch |

*(Continued)*

| Title page | |
| --- | --- |
| **Title of pages/slides** | **Description of content of pages/slides** |
| Business card | Design a business card to hand out to your networks |
| Pages/slides which set some objectives and an action plan | |
| Career goals | Outline your goals for each of the following:<br>• Short-term goals: for the first 6 months after graduating<br>• Medium-term goals: for the first 2 to 5 years of your career<br>• Long-term goals: 5 years from your graduation date |
| Action plan | List the actions you need to take to achieve the above goals. Add a timescale for each of your actions. Try to make this action plan achievable |
| Pages/slides which draw conclusions and set recommendations for the career plan | |
| Conclusions | Describe what you have learned from working on your career plan |
| Recommendations | Write some recommendations in the form of a 'to-do' list |
| End pages/slides | |
| References | List all the websites and other research sources you visited in the making of the career plan. These will be useful to refer back to at a later date |

Having set out the checklist above we will now work through each of the pages/slides in detail.

## Career Preferences

Return to Chapter 2 where we asked you to think about what sort of career you would like to pursue. Describe and analyse your aspirations in terms of salary level, work culture and future career progression. You should also consider what you learned about potential career areas from the career case study exercise in Chapter 4.

## Jobs Shortlist

For this section you should revisit the mock job hunt exercise that you carried out in preparation for the career case study in Chapter 4. Write a shortlist of job titles or freelance opportunities that would appeal to you. List some of the key words that are used to describe the jobs you are interested in. This will help you when it comes to using filters when searching for jobs online.

## Places of Work

For this section, you should state where you would like to work. For example, what country, county or city. List your preferences and give reasons for your choices.

It may be that you want to stay in the location of your university, or you may want to return to your hometown. Alternatively, you may decide to move to places where the jobs you are most interested in are concentrated. According to Nesta (nesta.org. uk), most creative jobs in the UK are clustered around London and in the Southeast, although there has been an increase in creative jobs in the Northwest of England (Sleeman, 2016). Either way, you will need to carry out research into where you choose to base yourself.

Start by researching if there is a creative or media hub located in the place you are interested in. Search online using terms such as: 'creative hub [insert place name]', 'creative quarter [insert place name]', 'media hub [insert place name]', 'cultural quarter [insert place name]'.

You can also search for different locations on the Adzuna website (adzuna.co.uk) by typing in the job title of interest followed by your preferred location. This will reveal direct matches between jobs and locations, or places close by.

If you are interested in working in another country, the following websites will be useful to you:

- GoinGlobal (online.goinglobal.com) – can be used for international job searches with country-specific information. You will need to create an account to access this resource
- Prospects (prospects.ac.uk) – search for the section on working abroad for detailed information about how to get a job, visa information, the language requirements and etiquette of the country, lists of industries and major companies. There are also links to jobs websites for the country of interest

Once you have researched thoroughly about your preferred places of work, you should summarise what you have found in your career plan.

## Potential Employers

List some employers and organisations you would like to work with and say why each one appeals to you. For self-employment, you can identify a business that you would like to emulate and state your reasons. You could also list companies you would like to approach for freelance work. For each organisation listed, summarise the company information, ethos and include a link to their website and social media. Gathering such information in one place on your career plan will help you when it comes to applying for and being interviewed for jobs as all the relevant information will be in one handy place.

## Key Messages

Create some key messages that you want potential employers to know about you. If you intend to work for yourself, this exercise may be key to your success. Include messages about your experience, your skills, your personality and your unique selling point. You can refer to the exercises in Chapter 3 where you analysed the skills and qualities that employers are looking for and performed a skills and qualities audit. This information will assist you when it comes to applying for jobs and being interviewed.

## Sources for Job Adverts

In Chapter 4 we advised you on where you might look for jobs in your area of interest. In the exercise about performing a mock job hunt by researching job roles within the media and creative industries, we supplied a list of websites where relevant jobs are listed. Revisit this exercise so you can add the various sources for jobs adverts – job websites, LinkedIn, company websites, and networks – to your career plan.

## Examples of Jobs

For this section of the career plan, you should include screen shots of live jobs you have found online. Include a copy of the advert, the job description and the person specification. If working for yourself, look for examples of potential clients or freelance opportunities that you can paste in here. This may even be an appropriate time for you to consider making an application!

## Further Study

Here you should give details of any further study you intend to undertake. It could include a postgraduate course (such as a Master's or PhD), vocational industry accredited courses, training schemes and apprenticeships.

Postgraduate courses give you the opportunity to specialise in a particular area of interest to gain further qualifications that may enhance your future job prospects. You can search online for postgraduate courses in your area of interest, and you are likely to find websites with lists of suitable universities and courses. You can use the Postgraduate Search website (postgraduatesearch.com) to search by subject (for example, Public Relations, Media, Documentary, Digital Media, Marketing). It is worth checking out the careers information related to the course. Find out whether there is any work experience included and the relevance of the course to your future career ambitions. Once you have found the courses that interest you, make a note of the dates of open day events and the deadlines for making your application.

Another possibility on graduation is to apply for a trainee scheme or apprenticeship for an organisation such as BBC, ITV and Channel 4. You can search for options from the following websites, but look for your own examples by searching for 'training scheme in [job area]', which will reveal a large number of opportunities across many areas of the industry:

- ScreenSkills (screenskills.com) – go to the search button and type in 'find an apprenticeship' where you will be given a comprehensive list of links and information on available opportunities
- The BBC Kick Start scheme (bbc.co.uk/careers, Instagram @BBCGETIN) – the BBC provides training schemes in journalism, production, design, engineering and technology, or the business aspects of the BBC, and they are open for graduates to apply
- 4Skills (careers.channel4.com/4skills) – this website has information on apprenticeships and production training schemes for Channel 4 or the independent production companies they work with

Another form of further study is the Graduate Development Programme or trainee scheme. These are structured training programmes run by an employer that usually last between one and two years. You are paid a salary and the programmes can improve your chances of gaining a job in the industry. You can visit the Prospects website (prospects.ac.uk) for more information, search for graduate schemes and click on Marketing and Media. Most of the available schemes are in marketing rather than media, though.

On your career plan, make a note of the schemes you are interested in. It is a good idea to create a timeline that includes details such as deadline dates for applications and course starting dates.

The next section of your career plan involves you in considering what you have to offer employers.

## Interests, Skills and Strengths

Describe and analyse your interests, skills and strengths in relation to your future career. These can be drawn from your degree course, life experience, hobbies, extra-curricular and work experience. You can gather this information from your current CV, online portfolio and professional social media. It will be useful for you to be able to match these skills and strengths with qualities and attributes listed in job adverts.

## Education

In this section write a summary of your education to date and evaluate how you will use it to contribute to your future career. It will be very useful here to identify what you have gained from your degree course so far. You should refer to specific projects, modules or coursework that provide evidence of your employability. You can use it when making your job applications and preparing for interviews.

## Work Experience

In this section you should detail all the relevant work experience you have had to date. Refer to Chapter 12 where you reflected on your work experience by writing a report. Summarise your reflections on the roles you undertook, the skills you gained or enhanced, the personal qualities you developed and the recommendations for future action that you made.

In the next subsection of your career plan, review and refine your resources for making job applications – your CV, cover letter/email, referees and professional branding.

## CV and Cover Letter/Email

Start by reviewing and updating your CV and cover letter/email and adding these to your career plan. Add details of any work experience or live/client-led projects you have undertaken. Keep this as a template that you can adapt for each application you make. Your university careers department will often provide feedback if you ask for it. You may find it useful to refresh your memory on developing your CV and cover letter/email by revisiting Chapter 7. You may also want to consider whether producing or updating a video CV is appropriate for you.

## Referees

You most probably have a statement 'referees available on request' or similar at the end of your CV. Now is a good time to decide on who you would like to ask to be your referees and to gain their permission. It is helpful to prepare notes on what you would like them to mention in their reference for you and to record these notes in your career plan. In this context, a reference is a written statement about your qualifications, character and suitability for a position.

It is important you ask permission from your potential referees *before* you make applications for jobs. You will usually have two referees, but sometimes three. It depends on what is asked for in a job advert or application form.

- Your first referee – is usually an academic one. It may be a tutor from your degree course, your personal tutor, your dissertation supervisor or a tutor who has taught you a lot and who knows you well
- Your second referee – is usually an employer from your work experience or paid work
- Your third referee – is not usually required, but may be useful to have one in reserve. It should be someone who can provide a different perspective about you from the other two referees

Ensure that whoever you ask is willing and able to give you a good reference, for example, a course leader, personal tutor, dissertation supervisor or someone who knows you well.

For an employer/placement provider or client, you may want to consider somebody who previously gave you some good feedback.

You can start by producing a database with the following details:

- the full name and title (Ms, Mrs, Mr, Dr, Prof, etc.) of each referee
- the job title and company/organisation they work for, including the company website
- their relationship to you and basic details of why you have chosen them to act as one of your referees
- their work email address
- their professional social media addresses
- whether and when they agreed to give you a reference

Ask their permission in good time and never put your referee's name down without asking for (and receiving) permission from them in advance. It goes without saying that your request for a reference should be made in as polite and professional way as possible. Use the list of tips and hints below to help achieve this:

- start by telling the referee that you are contacting them because you are asking them if they are willing to act as one of your referees
- provide a time scale to give them a sense of when their reference will be needed
- explain the sorts of jobs you are likely to be applying for
- give the referee some information to remind them of how they know you (for example, the course or module you studied, or the work experience you had with them)

It is probably best to send your request as an email which observes the following email etiquette (revisit Chapter 11 for a refresher to help with this):

- address your email appropriately
- make use of full sentences
- check your spelling
- avoid being over familiar or too casual
- avoid appearing rushed in your contact with them
- be positive and honest about your strengths and weaknesses

Once your referee has agreed, you should provide them with the following in a single email:

- a reminder that they have agreed to be one of your referees
- details of the job you are applying for
- the skills and qualities that are required for the job in question and some evidence of you having acquired these
- what you feel you have achieved both academically and otherwise while at university, including evidence of your strengths
- a link to your CV, your online portfolio and your professional social media

The following list itemises what employers might ask your referee to comment on:

- how long they have known you and in what capacity
- whether your skillset is appropriate to the job, for example technical skills, interpersonal and teamwork skills, written and spoken communication skills, including presentation skills
- your personal qualities, such as your level of creativity, your reliability, attendance and punctuality, your ability to work to a brief, your ability to work under pressure, your organisation and time management abilities, your levels of motivation, maturity, self-discipline and honesty, your ability to take responsibility, show commitment and work well with others
- your participation in university life, extra-curricular engagement, your academic record and your predicted or actual degree result
- whether they feel you are suitable for the job being applied for
- finally, whether they would recommend you to the employer

## Professional Branding

You should include links on your career plan to the professional social media and online portfolios, websites and blogs that you have developed. You are also advised to update the content where appropriate. For example, add details of any work experience you have engaged in and any recommendations or testimonials you have received from employers or clients.

Now is also a good time to update your professional headshot. Ask a peer to help you with producing a head-and-shoulders portrait that constructs your professional identity. You should be appropriately dressed so that you can use the photo across all of your professional social media. It is advisable to use the same image across all the platforms that you use as this will give consistency to your brand.

In your career plan, think of three key messages that you want your professional branding to communicate (or convey) about you. Compose three sentences to reflect these messages and add them to your career plan.. Also, identify your unique selling point. Perhaps you can ask your mentor or one of your peers to make some suggestions to help you with this task.

The next section in your career plan concerns your networking.

## Your Networks

Think about the current network that you can consider as being the basis of your professional network going forward. Create a list that makes up your professional network. You don't necessarily have to be known to these people, just to have some professional connection to them. It can include:

- work experience employers from any work experience or placements you have done

- the person or people you interviewed for your career case study in Chapter 4
- employers from jobs you have had (where they are appropriate to your career ambition)
- alumni of your degree course. You can find these through your university careers department or your tutor. You can also use the LinkedIn alumni application, where you can search for graduates of your degree course and find out what they are doing now
- current peers, who may well be your future work colleagues or part of your wider networks
- contacts via your professional social media
- the professional networking organisations that you found through working on your career case study in Chapter 4
- university tutors and other staff, such as your careers advisors

Sort this list into a database of contacts. For each contact you can detail how they may be able to help you gain or make progress in your future employment. Make sure that you are linked to them on your professional social media accounts.

You can build on this by choosing from your database one or two people who may be willing to act as a mentor for you in your early career. This can range from establishing an informal connection where they give you some general careers advice to having regular catch-ups to discuss your progress. Such contact might include:

- advice on the content of your CV, professional social media and online portfolio
- tips and hints on working in the sector and advice on any professional networks and associations that would be useful to you
- advice on where to look for jobs in their sector and whether they know of any suitable openings
- advice on available internships, training courses and **job shadowing** opportunities
- tips and hints on applying for and being interviewed for jobs and the possibility of having some interview practice with them

An especially useful way of building your network is to explore where graduates of your degree course have ended up working. We have suggested that you can use the LinkedIn alumni application or your careers service and course tutors to locate alumni from your degree. Once you have made contact, you can ask them some of the following questions:

- What are your most abiding memories from your time at university?
- What skills and qualities did you gain on your degree that have been useful in your career?
- How has any work experience you did on your degree influenced your career?
- What did you take from your university experience into the world of work?
- What was your biggest surprise/challenge when you went into the world of work?
- What advice would you have given your just-about-to-graduate self?

## Networking

In most parts of the media and creative industries there is a heavy reliance on networking as a way of finding jobs and opportunities or advancing your career. It is a way of meeting like-minded people, finding inspiration, information and advice and sourcing ideas. It can also provide opportunities to collaborate with others in the sector.

You can find opportunities for networking online or in person through events such as conferences, careers fairs, employability events, training courses and through attending employer presentations. You can engage with networking online through organisations such as those listed below, and it is worth searching for organisations specific to your own interest area too:

- The Creative Industries Federation (creativeindustriesfederation.com) – a networking and campaigning organisation for the creative industries
- Creative Pool (creativepool.com) – a networking organisation for the creative sector
- Mama Youth (mamayouth.org.uk) – a support and networking organisation for young people from diverse communities wanting to enter the media industry
- Production Base (productionbase.co.uk) – a networking organisation for freelancers
- The Radio Academy (radioacademy.org) – a networking organisation for people working in radio
- The TV Collective (thetvcollective.org) – a group supporting filmmakers from diverse backgrounds to connect with each other
- TIGA (tiga.org) – a network for games developers and digital publishers and the trade association representing the video games industry
- Triforce Creative Network (thetcn.com) – a networking organisation for the broadcast media industry
- Women in Film and Television Network (wftv.org.uk) – a membership organisation supporting women in the media and creative sector

Any networking activity should begin with a plan. First, decide what you want to get out of it. This can include:

- a job or opening
- some training
- some ideas and inspiration
- people to collaborate with
- some advice

Next, prepare some tools to support your networking. This can include an elevator pitch to introduce yourself and a business card to leave with people you are networking with. These tools will help you to talk about yourself with confidence.

# Elevator Pitch

It is important in the early days of your career to have an elevator pitch ready to support your networking. You have experience of preparing an elevator pitch in Chapter 9 where it was used to assist you in gaining freelance work for your work experience. In the context of networking, the elevator pitch is an introductory summary about you that will help you to achieve your goals for networking. It will help you if you can articulate concisely why you are attending the event and what you want to achieve from the event. The following structure for your 60–90-second pitch may be a useful guide:

- your name and specialism – for example, a videographer looking for work in the freelance sector, a marketing specialist looking for a mentor
- why you are here, what you want to achieve – for example, to find collaborators, to get some advice, to look for employment opportunities
- your unique selling point (USP) – a skill, personal quality or experience that you have to offer
- explain why they should consider you for what they have to offer – for example, as a potential employee or collaborator
- close your elevator pitch with a 'call to action' – for example, sharing a copy of your CV or business card, swapping contact details via professional social media, or arranging a follow-up meeting

# Business Card

You can support your networking and your elevator pitch by producing a business card. A business card should include a logo or image, your name, job title or area of specialism, your phone number and/or email address, your website address, and links to your professional social media. You can use a QR code for this. You can also invent a slogan that summarises the unique selling point you have identified in your elevator pitch.

The closing sections of your career plan are where you outline your goals and action plan.

# Career Goals

In the section of your career plan that outlines your goals, you should think about your short-term goals for the first six months after graduating, your medium-term goals, which are where you would like to be within two to five years, and your long-term goals, which look forward to five years from your graduation date.

Your goals can cover:

- gaining qualifications, further education and training, including continuing professional development (CPD)
- developing skills

- gaining experience
- specifying certain achievements to be met
- setting milestones in terms of employment and career progression
- establishing a portfolio of work and projects
- developing personal skills and qualities

In your career plan, you should elaborate the above goals and set out the specific details of what you want to achieve.

## Action Plan

You should now list the actions you need to take to achieve the goals you have specified in your plan. Include a timescale for each of your actions. Try to make your action plan achievable and as realistic as possible. You might find it easier to do this if you write it from the end point and work backwards to the present day. You can create it as a timeline to help you visualise it.

The final section of your career plan draws conclusions and sets out recommendations.

## Conclusions, Recommendations and References

Having reached the end of your career plan, you should review the document as a whole and reflect on what you have learned from working on it. For example, you may have learned that the employment area you intend to pursue is much more extensive than you anticipated, and that further training, qualifications and experience might be required.

You should follow up your review by setting yourself some recommended actions. This can be in the form of a 'to-do' list. For example, you may identify the need to apply for further training or to undertake more work experience to achieve your goals.

Finally, the last section should be a reference list of all the websites and sources you have used in the making of the career plan. You never know when you might want to return to these resources in the future for further career research and planning.

# Conclusion

In this chapter we have encouraged you to create a career plan. Doing so will help you to build on your existing research into career areas that you are interested in.

It is important to recognise that your career plan is a dynamic; it is a constantly evolving tool that should be revisited and revised throughout your early career.

Imagine the fascination of re-reading the career plan you have just produced ten years from now!

Let us give the final words of advice and support to a selection of the media and creative industries experts we have heard from throughout this book.

## Hear from the Experts

"Don't jump into the first job that you find. There's always time. You have to figure out what you like the most. You have to summarise everything that you have, every experience that you gained. Take some time off and start investigating what you like the most, what you have the most passion for."

*– Eugene Kogut, Videographer*

"Try and ignore this massive pressure to get your dream job as your first job, because it doesn't happen to most people. It definitely didn't happen for me. My first job was actually as a Production Assistant, it wasn't a creative role. But it was actually a great springboard for my creative career. I still use a lot of the skills and knowledge that I gained from that role every day, even though I now do a creative job. But it was a great way to learn – by being in the industry all day, every day, being surrounded by animation and working with clients and creative teams. Don't turn your nose up at roles like that because they can be really helpful and you can make connections with people. I've since done creative work for the animation studio that I was a Production Assistant at. So all of those connections can lead to things later on in your career."

*– Em Green, Motion Designer, Alive With Ideas*

"When it came to working with DeCantillon, I worked on the marketing for the film and then when the next project started, I was asked by the team which department I wanted to work in. They were giving me a full opportunity to choose which route I wanted to take. I just said 'get me on set doing anything'. I will do anything because it's experience and I know the team will appreciate any help I can give. I will always be grateful to the DeCantillon team for this and for giving me my first film credit. What's even more great is that I can follow my other passions and projects, like *Flavour of the Film*, at the same time. It gives you room to explore and grow, as well as gain experience in the industry at the same time."

*– Laura Savage, Marketing Director, DeCantillon Films*

"Do not put too much pressure on yourself. I think sometimes you can put way too much pressure on yourself and you think 'I'm going to come out of university and I'm going to walk straight into a job'. The reality is that it's not always like that. Some people will go straight into employment. But I think it's about being assured enough to know that something is going to come your way. You've got this far. It feels like quite a leap to go from university to employment. So, I would say don't put too much pressure on yourself because something's going to come along and it's all going to work out. Yeah, give yourself a break!"

*– Eugene Kogut, Videographer*

"I took a gap year and I bartended for a year. Taking that time between, although it can be horrendous and you think, 'oh, I'm never going to get a job, I'm still looking, I'm not getting any responses.' It's so important to take that time to consider 'what do I actually want from my 40-year career that's looming ahead of me?' And so, I realised I wanted to do more education.

I wanted to do a Master's. I wanted to work with agencies. Taking that time to think about where you're going next is incredibly useful and there's no shame in bartending or doing something else while you job search. Saying 'I'm an artist but I bartend' still makes you an artist."

*– Shauna Wilkinson, Creative, Ginger Root*

"I found that starting at a smaller business is a really nice introduction to the workplace. You get to learn, and they get to help you out even more because you're not just a cog in the machine. Just get your name out there, reach out to companies. Even if you don't turn out to get the job, it's beneficial for them to get to know you. Making relationships and introducing oneself is always a smart idea."

*– Alexa Garcia Degante, Account Executive, Framework Design*

"I remember being at university and editing a project you could take two weeks, three weeks. In my work, I'm just working on something now where I've gone out and shot something on the Wednesday and I've got to edit it all and get a first version to the client within a day. That's definitely been the biggest challenge adjusting to that, but I'm really enjoying it."

*– Sam Reynolds, Video and Motion Producer, Adtrak*

"The biggest surprise is the difference in how you're treated compared to something like a part-time job. It might seem obvious that a part-time job in retail and hospitality there will be some difference. But when you experience that firsthand, managers not giving you the freedom. It's such a huge amount of trust placed in you working in a job in the industry where you're just kind of left to your own devices and you're entrusted with getting the work done. You're not micromanaged as you would be in hospitality or retail. So that's the biggest surprise."

*– Sam Reynolds, Video and Motion Producer, Adtrak*

"Based on 20 plus years recruitment experience, you've got to position yourself right in front of potential employers. And the way to do that is you're going to have to be proactive. You're going to have to do some research, find businesses that do the stuff that you are interested in and be quite broad. Don't just focus in on your dream job, think of all the possibilities where your skills are relevant. You follow them on social media and you drop them an email. It doesn't matter if it goes through to a contact box on the website. They're a small business. They'll still see it. All you need to say to them is 'Hi, looked at your work. Love what you do. I'm going to be finishing my education soon and would love to be talking to an organisation like you. The next time you have an opportunity please, can we talk?' You don't need to say any more than that. Send them your CREATEBritain profile, a portfolio, CV, or links to your website. Tell them you're flexible. Tell them you're ambitious. And tell them you would love to be the first person they speak to the next time they need some support. You've now positioned yourself bench strength, flexible resource, giving them the confidence to pursue growth and within a couple of months you'll probably get a call."

*– Richard Woods, Co-founder, CREATEBritain.com*

"Work more and study more and if you have opportunities just do it and bear in mind that whatever you do, you do it right. Do it for yourself. You don't do it for your mom or your dad or your girlfriend. You just do for yourself. That's very important."

*– Eugene Kogut, Videographer*

"You only get one chance sometimes in life for an opportunity, so make it count. Be the driving force behind your own destiny. Work hard, stay focused and positive."

*– Radha Singh, CEO/Creative Director, THE HOUSE OF RADHA*

"Leave a lasting and positive impression as an intern. This is really important because in the future, if there is ever an opportunity to apply for a role full-time with that business, then that positive impression is only going to help with your application. Be proactive, be positive and be friendly because the employer will remember you for all of those good reasons. We have interns with us all year round and I always remember the ones that have left a positive, lasting impression on me."

*– Tom Walters, Account Director*

"I wouldn't worry if people don't know what they want to do when they grow up, because I still don't know what I really want to do when I grow up. But I'm enjoying this at the moment. I would certainly say if you've got an open mind then speak to people like us and see what we can do."

*– Simon Elliott, Managing Director, Diversity Agency*

---

## Further Reading

Angone, Paul (2018) *101 Questions You Need to Ask in Your Twenties (and Let's Be Honest in Your Thirties Too)*. Chicago, IL: Moody Publishers. Aimed at graduates and people in their twenties and thirties, this book has a section on careers.

Scott, Susan (2017a) *How to Have an Outstanding Career, and Become the Person You've Always Dreamed of Being*. The Young Professional's Guide. Croydon, UK: Filament Publishing. Using the concept of a 'resilient career', this book assists you in recognising talents for a job while maintaining your wellbeing.

Scott, Susan (2017b) *How to Prevent Burnout, and Reignite Your Life and Career*. The Young Professional's Guide. Croydon, UK: Filament Publishing. In this book, Scott gives advice on your life and career and provides tips on how to avoid stress.

Sleeman, Cath (2016, February 1) 'Where do creatives cluster?' *TheLong+Short* [website]. https://thelongandshort.org/creativity/where-do-creatives-cluster.html. This is an interesting article that provides an insight into where jobs in the creative industries are clustered around the UK.

# GLOSSARY

**Active listening** – A process of listening in which you give visual and verbal signals to the person speaking that you have listened carefully and noted what they have said. This can include making eye contact, nodding and verbally summarising what the person has said.

**Alumni** – Graduates or former students of your degree course.

**Assertiveness** – A quality in which a person can exude confidence with a positive, can-do attitude.

**Autonomy** – An opportunity for taking charge of your own decision-making and actions in the workplace, rather than only taking orders.

**BECTU** – The Broadcasting, Entertainment, Communications and Theatre Union, a union for creative workers.

**Behaviours** – The way you act or present yourself (as opposed to skills that you have learned).

**Branding** – *See* professional branding

**Career case study** – An investigation into a career area.

**Career plan** – A tool for assessing your skills and interests, setting career goals and developing a plan of action.

**Career portfolio** – A portfolio of evidence of your skills and experience used for job applications or for showcasing your skills when networking for freelance work. It may be a hard copy or more usually produced as a website.

**Client-led** – A project in which a client provides the brief for your work.

**Commercial sector awareness** – An attribute for understanding how industries work, what is going on in the world, and how it might impact the future.

**Communication skills** – Skills in achieving communicative goals via particular communication behaviours (such as giving oral presentations or composing emails).

**Continuing professional development (CPD)** – A process of noting, reflecting and continually enhancing skills gained in the workplace which give an employee a sense of progression and achievement.

**Corporate social responsibility (CSR)** – A management concept that helps a company to integrate social and environmental concerns and be accountable to its stakeholders.

**Cover letter/cover email** – A letter or email than accompanies a copy of an applicant's CV in a job application. It outlines what the applicant is applying for and the main reasons for their application.

**Creative industries** – The creative industries are a wide range of sectors including jobs for writers, musicians, content creators and public relations officers. The industries have their origin in creativity, skill and talent.

**Creativity and innovation** – An attribute for offering ideas and solutions to challenges from new and unique angles and putting those ideas into action.

**Critical analysis** – A skill in assessing the quality of evidence in scholarship to decide whether it can support your argument.

**Critical reflection** – A skill in thinking objectively about situations and experiences, analysing and learning from them.

**Cultural awareness** – An awareness and acceptance of other cultures and colleagues' cultural identities in the workplace and wider community.

**Curriculum vitae (CV)** – A document used to show potential employers details about you, including your skills, experience and qualifications.

**Debriefing** – An evaluation that takes place after a piece of work has been finished to determine what went well and what can be improved.

**Digital footprint** – The online presence you create by your posts on various social media platforms.

**Digital marketing** – Promoting or selling a service or product via content creation, social media and websites.

**Diversity** – A group of people in the workplace who come from a variety of ethnic, socio-economic and cultural backgrounds, and who also have differing experiences and interests.

**DoP (Director of Photography)** – A term given to a camera operator who is responsible for framing shots and lighting a scene.

**Elevator pitch** – A short pitch, usually lasting for between 30 and 90 seconds. This is a useful way of presenting ideas or 'selling' a service in a concise and dynamic way.

**Email etiquette** – The use of appropriate and polite registers and language to achieve professional communications via email.

**Emotional intelligence** – Having the ability to see how others might see you and acting accordingly in professional situations.

**Employability** – The skillset and personal qualities required for the world of work.

**Enterprising** – Having the initiative and drive to recognise opportunities and the motivation to carry this through.

**Entrepreneurship** – A risk-taking action in setting up new enterprises for profit. An entrepreneur is willing to try out new and unusual ways of achieving something.

**Equality, diversity and inclusion (EDI) awareness** – A quality for recognising and understanding protected characteristics (for example, gender, ethnicity, disability, LGBTQ+) and making people feel welcomed and valued.

**Extra-curricular** – Character-building pursuits outside study or university projects that can be cited in job applications (e.g. sports which can enhance teamworking skills).

**Freelancing** – A type of work where the worker is not committed to a single, long-term employer or customer, but lends their skills to numerous clients on a flexible basis.

**Functional skills** – Practical, day-to-day skills that allow individuals to operate effectively and independently in the workplace. *See also* skills, hard and soft skills, generic skills, key skills and transferable skills.

**GDPR (General Data Protection Regulation) statement** – A statement that gives permission for a personal document, such as your CV, to be distributed to potential employers other than the recipient that you have sent it to.

**Generic skills** – The name given to all-purpose skills which can be applied in a wide range of tasks and job contexts, such as motivation, teamworking and problem-solving. *See also* skills, hard and soft skills, functional skills, key skills and transferable skills.

**Glass ceiling** – A sometimes invisible barrier to success that people come across in their careers.

**Graduate employment/graduate jobs** – A level of employment aimed at university leavers.

**Hard skills and soft skills** – Hard skills are practical and technical skills such as proficiency in editing software, whereas soft skills refer to employability skills such as motivation, communication and showing initiative. *See also* skills, functional skills, generic skills, key skills and transferable skills.

**Human Resources (HR)** – In an organisation, this is a department in charge of all employees and employer-related operations.

**Internship** – A professional learning experience that offers meaningful, practical work related to a student's field of study.

**Interpersonal skills** – A set of skills which are demonstrated when interacting with other people, such as teamwork, social skills, communication skills, cultural skills, leadership and management skills.

**Job sector** – A classification of a broad group of occupations or industries that are related to each other. There are several job sectors within the broad umbrella of the media and creative industries.

**Job shadowing** – Working alongside or observing and gaining insight into the role and duties of an employee.

**Key skills** – A particular set of skills required for a range of activities in work and wider life. *See also* skills, hard and soft skills, functional skills, generic skills and transferable skills.

**Leadership and management** – An attribute for influencing and motivating others to achieve a common goal.

**LinkedIn** – A professional networking social media application.

**Locus of control** – Being able to control your own destiny; used in the context of entrepreneurship.

**Marketing** – *See* digital marketing

**Mindfulness** – A way of paying attention, in the moment, to whatever thoughts, feelings or bodily sensations we are experiencing, and using this as a relaxation tool to de-clutter our thoughts.

**Mock interview** – A practice interview. This can be conducted with another person who will give you feedback, or with an online application which will analyse your performance.

**Networking** – Meeting and interacting with like-minded people, potential employers or clients. Networking can stretch your experience and broaden your horizons. It is also a way of finding future work collaborators, clients or customers.

**Pay gap** – An unfair difference between the pay awarded to two different sectors of the population.

**Person specification** – A list of selection criteria for the ideal candidate for a job. This includes skills, qualities, attributes, experience and qualifications, which are usually categorised as 'essential' or 'desirable'.

**Personality traits** – Features defined by your characteristic feelings and behaviours. Employers often list personality traits in job adverts or look for evidence of them in applications and interviews.

**Placement** – A work placement is a period of supervised work for an employer or organisation, usually completed during term time as part of a course. *See also* work experience.

**Placement report** – A report written to reflect on and demonstrate what you have learned or gained from taking a work placement.

**Portfolio career** – Working freelance in a variety of roles rather than just one long-term job in one organisation.

**Proactive** – The ability to create or initiate a situation rather than wait for instruction.

**Problem-solving** – A skill in responding to and managing unexpected situations or challenges.

**Professional associations** – Groups that support the interests of people and organisations in a particular profession. *See also* sector networks and support organisations

**Professional branding** – An employer-facing or potential customer-facing digital footprint that conveys an appropriately professional image of yourself.

**Project management** – An attribute for the use of knowledge, skills and techniques to result in a deliverable outcome.

**Protected characteristics** – These are characteristics defined by the Equality Act (2010) as being age, gender, race, disability, religion or belief, sexual orientation, gender reassignment, marriage or civil partnership, pregnancy or maternity.

**Psychometric tests** – Tests used in the process of recruiting and interviewing for jobs. An objective way to measure a candidate's potential for success in a job role. They measure one's personality and a range of skills, abilities and knowledge. *See also* Verbal reasoning test and situational judgement

**Public Relations (PR)** – Communications that build, maintain and manage the reputation of an organisation.

**Qualities and attributes** – Characteristics or traits natural to a person (as opposed to skills which are learned through education, training or work, for example).

**Referee** – The title given to somebody who gives you a reference for your job applications.

**Reference** – A recommendation given to you by a tutor or previous employer to aid your job applications. A reference is usually passed directly from the referee to your potential employer and confirms aspects of your character, such as attendance, reliability and work ethic.

**Remote working** – Work that takes place away from a central office provided by your employer, usually at home.

**Resilience** – A demonstration of coping skills and the ability to adapt to challenging situations.

**Sector** – *See* job sector

**Sector networks** – Network organisations that offer support and guidance to people working within a particular sector. They are a useful way of making contact with like-minded professionals. *See also* support organisations and professional associations.

**Self-awareness** – Used in discussions of emotional intelligence to gauge a person's knowledge of themselves and how others perceive them.

**Self-employment** – A general term given to any type of work which is generated by a worker rather than an employer (e.g. freelance work, small business ownership, entrepreneurship).

**Showreel** – A montage of extracts of audio-visual work to show prospective employers.

**Situational judgement** – How a person responds to workplace scenarios. *See also* psychometric tests.

**Skills** – Expertise learned through education, work, training or life experience. *See also* hard and soft skills, functional skills, generic skills, key skills and transferable skills.

**Skills audit** – Creating a checklist and assessing your existing skills.

**Small to medium-sized enterprise (SME)** – An organisation that has fewer than 250 employees. This can be broken down further into micro enterprise (fewer than 10 employees), small enterprise (fewer than 50 employees) and medium (fewer than 250 employees).

**SMART (Specific, Measurable, Achievable, Relevant, Time-bound) objectives** – A technique for ensuring that your objectives are based on criteria that make your goals meaningful.

**Soft Skills** – *See* hard skills and soft skills

**Support organisations** – In the media and creative industries this is an organisation that may support a particular demographic or people within a particular industry sector (e.g. women working in film, or educators working in film and media). *See also* sector networks and professional associations.

**STAR(R) – (Situation, Task, Action, Result, Reflection) technique** – A technique used in job interviews to ensure that answers to questions are detailed and reflective.

**Strengths** – How a person demonstrates the durability required for a particular role.

**Sustainability awareness** – An attribute for ensuring a balance between economic growth, environmental care and social wellbeing for current and future generations.

**Teamwork** – A skill in working effectively and collaboratively with others.

**Testimonial** – A formal statement testifying to someone's character, experience and qualifications.

**Time management** – A skill in using and organising time productively and efficiently.

**Trade association** – A group or association of people in a particular industry or sector with common interests.

**Trade press** – Niche publications associated with a particular trade. These can be in print, online or a combination of the two.

**Trade union** – An organisation that negotiates fair wages and working conditions for members of that union.

**Transferable skills** – The employability skills that you can apply from one context to another (e.g. from a university project to a professional workplace). *See also* skills, hard and soft skills, functional skills, generic skills and key skills.

**Verbal reasoning test** – Evaluating the logic of a given statement. *See also* psychometric tests.

**VFX (visual effects)** – A process of creating computer generated imagery such as 3D modelling or green screen video production.

**Work experience** – Experience of work which can be conducted in several ways including job shadowing, volunteering, and working to a client brief. Work experience can also be conducted more formally as a structured, employer-led placement. *See also* placement.

**Work–life balance** – The healthy balance between fulfilling your work duties and being able to meet friends and family, sleep well and eat well.

**Work placement** – *See* placement

**Working to a brief** – A skill in following instructions to a shared purpose.

**Work-related learning (WRL)** – Structured opportunities for learning, achieved through authentic activity and supervised in the workplace.

# BIBLIOGRAPHY

Angone, Paul (2018) *101 Questions You Need to Ask in Your Twenties (and Let's Be Honest in Your Thirties Too)*. Chicago, IL: Moody Publishers.

BBC (n.d.) *BBC Careers* [website]. Available at: https://careers.bbc.co.uk/

Becker, Lucinda (2020) *Write a Brilliant CV*. London: Sage.

BECTU (Broadcasting, Entertainment, Communications and Theatre Union) (n.d.) *Creative Toolkit*. London: BECTU. Available at: creativetoolkit.org.uk

Beverland, Michael (2021) *Brand Management: Co-creating Meaningful Brands*. London: Sage.

Blalock, Becky (2013) *Dare: Straight Talk on Confidence, Courage, and Career for Women in Charge*. London: John Wiley and Sons.

Caird, Sally (1990) 'What does it mean to be enterprising?' British Journal of Management, 1(3), 137–145. http://dx.doi.org/10.1111/j.1467-8551.1990.tb00002.x

Creative Industries Federation (n.d.) *Creative Industries Jobs – Risks and Opportunities*. London: CFI. Available at: www.creativeindustriesfederation.com/sites/default/files/2017-09/Creative%20industries%20workforce.pdf

Culver, Sherri Hop, and Seguin, James (2018) *Media Career Guide: Preparing for Jobs in the 21st Century*. Boston, MA and New York: Bedford Books.

Dass, Matthew, Goodwin, Andrew, Wood, Melissa, and Luanaigh, Aoife (2015) *Sector Insights: Skills Challenges in the Digital and Creative Sector*. UK Commission for Employment Skills report. London: UK Commission for Employment Skills.

Davies, Gill, and Balkwill, Richard (2011) *The Professional's Guide to Publishing: A Practical Introduction to Working in the Publishing Industry*. London: Kogan Page.

Davies, Rosamund, and Sigthorsson, Gauti (2013) *Introducing the Creative Industries: From Theory to Practice*. London: Sage.

DCMS (2015, January) 'Creative Industries Economic Estimates January 2015 – Key Findings', www.gov.uk/government/statistics/creative-industries-economic-estimates-january-2015/creative-industries-economic-estimates-january-2015-key-findings

Edwards, Julian (2022) *Write Reflectively*. London: Sage.

Eggert, Max (2010) *Body Language: Impress, Persuade and Succeed with the Power of Body Language*. London: Pearson Education.

Fanthome, Christine (2005) *Work Placements: A Survival Guide for Students*. London: Springer Nature.

Gallagher, Matt (2016) *Breaking into UK Film and Television Drama for New Entrants and Graduates*. Scotts Valley, CA: CreateSpace Independent Publishing Platform.

Goleman, Daniel (2004) *Emotional Intelligence and Working with Emotional Intelligence*. London: Bloomsbury.

Gov.uk (n.d.) 'Business and self-employed: Tools and guidance for business'. *Gov.uk* [website]. www.gov.uk/browse/business

Grade, Alison (2020) 'The Freelance Toolkit' (3rd edition). Available at: www.screenskills. com/media/4092/freelance-tooolkit-10122020.pdf

Gregory, Georgina., Healy, Ros, and Mazierska, Ewa (2007) *Careers in Media and Film: The Essential Guide*. London: Sage.

Hasson, Gill, and Butler, Donna (2020) *Mental Health and Wellbeing in the Workplace: A Practical Guide for Employers and Employees*. London: John Wiley and Sons.

Hatschek, Keith (2014) *How to Get a Job in the Music Industry*. Boston, MA: Berklee Press.

Helyer, R., and Lee, D. (2014) 'The role of work experience in the future employability of Higher Education graduates'. *Higher Education Quarterly*, 68(3), 348–372.

Hennessey, Brittany (2018) *Influencer: Building Your Personal Brand in the Age of Social Media*. New York: Citadel Press.

Hesmondhalgh, David (2019) *The Cultural Industries* (4th edition). London: Sage.

Innes, James (2016) *The Interview Book: How to Prepare and Perform at Your Best in Any Interview*. Harlow: Pearson Education.

Kerry, Matthew, and Stone, Georgia (2018) *Introducing Media Practice: The Essential Guide*. London: Sage.

Mair, David (2019) *The Student Guide to Mindfulness*. London: Sage.

Marwick, Alice (2015) *Status Update: Celebrity, Publicity, and Branding in the Social Media Age*. New Haven, CT: Yale University Press.

Mills, Corinne (2015) *You're Hired! CV: How to Write a Brilliant CV*. Bath: Trotman Indigo Publishing.

Moon, Jenny (2004) *A Handbook of Reflective and Experiential Learning: Theory and Practice*. London: Routledge.

Neugebauer, John, and Evans-Brian, Jane (2009) *Making the Most of Your Placement*. London: Sage.

Prospects (n.d.) *Prospects* [website]. www.prospects.ac.uk/

Ricketts, Gavin (2012) *TV Runner Handbook and CV Template*. London: Napoleon Creative Books.

Rook, Steve (2016) *Work Experience, Placements and Internships*. Palgrave Study Skills Series. Basingstoke: Palgrave Macmillan.

Rook, Steve (2019) *The Graduate Career Guidebook: Advice for Students and Graduates on Career Options, Jobs, Volunteering, Applications, Interviews, and Self-Employment*. Basingstoke: Palgrave Macmillan.

Scott, Susan (2017a) *How to Have an Outstanding Career, and Become the Person You've Always Dreamed of Being*. The Young Professional's Guide. Croydon, UK: Filament Publishing.

Scott, Susan (2017b) *How to Prevent Burnout, and Reignite Your Life and Career*. The Young Professional's Guide. Croydon, UK: Filament Publishing.

Sleeman, Cath (2016, February 1) 'Where do creatives cluster?' *The Long & Short* [website]. https://thelongandshort.org/creativity/where-do-creatives-cluster.html

Sleeman, Cath, and Windsor, George (2017, April 18) 'A closer look at creatives: Using job adverts to identify the skill needs of creative talent'. *Nesta* [website]. www.nesta. org.uk/blog/a-closer-look-at-creatives/

Smith, Jemma (2023, May) 'Create a great video CV'. *Prospects* [website]. www.prospects. ac.uk/careers-advice/cvs-and-cover-letters/create-a-great-video-cv

The Film and TV Charity (n.d.) *The Film and TV Charity* [website]. www.filmtvcharity.org.uk

The TV Watercooler (n.d.) *The TV Watercooler* [website]. https://tvwatercooler.org/

The TV Watercooler (n.d.) 'Tips for TV Runners'. *The TV Watercooler* [website]. https://tvwatercooler.org/latest/tips-for-tv-runners

The Unit List (2011) *The Unit List* [website]. theunitlist.com

TripleC (n.d.) 'The 5 As, Guidelines for Disability Inclusion in UK Television Production'. Available at: triplec.org.uk/wp-content/uploads/2022/10/The-5-As_FINAL_230822.pdf

Turton, Tora (2021) *Adzuna* [Blog]. www.adzuna.co.uk/blog/the-most-inclusive-lgbtq-cities-regions-sectors/

UK Commission for Employment and Skills (2015, June 9) *Sector Insights: Skills and Performance Challenges in the Digital and Creative Sector Report.* London: UKCES. Available at: www.gov.uk/government/publications/sector-insights-skills-and-performance-challenges-in-the-digital-and-creative-sector

Watson, Warren (2019) *Surviving Journalism: Fireproofing a Career in the Fourth Estate.* Portland, OR: Marion Street Press.

Williams, Lynn (2021) *Ultimate Interview: 100s of Sample Questions and Answers for Interview Success.* London: Kogan Page.

Work Foundation (2019, August 16) *Annual ScreenSkills Assessment: August 2019.* London and Lancaster: Work Foundation. Available at: www.screenskills.com/media/2853/2019-08-16-annual-screenskills-assessment.pdf

World Economic Forum (2020, October 20) *The Future of Jobs Report 2020.* Cologny, Switzerland: World Economic Forum. Available at: www.weforum.org/reports/the-future-of-jobs-report-2020/

# INDEX

**Note:** Page numbers followed by *t* indicate tables.